If you were ever a kid on a school bus...

If you are the parent of a kid on a school bus...

If you were ever a school bus driver...

If you are a school bus driver...

If you have ever been 'caught' behind a school bus when you have to get somewhere fast and... and...!

...then, this book is for you.

BUS
11
STO
Jenn Salmon 2010

A Year on The Bus

Dan Close

Illustrated by Jennifer Salmon

The Tamarac Press • Warren, Vermont
2010

The names of students, their family members and other members of the community have been changed to protect their privacy.

ISBN-13: 978-0-9706620-2-6

The Tamarac Press
Warren, VT
First Edition, First Printing
Fall 2010

This book is dedicated to the students of Underhill and Jericho who rode Bus 4 and 5 during the school years 2008-2009 and 2009-2010...

...and also to the dedicated School Bus Drivers of the Chittenden East Supervisory Union, serving the towns of Underhill, Jericho, Richmond, Bolton, and Huntington, Vermont

And especially to Phil and Pat Halsey

THE YEAR

A Word about this Book

A Year on the Bus reflects the lives of contemporary school students from kindergarten to twelfth grade who live in the rolling hill country of northern Vermont. It also reflects the life of their bus driver and the times in which we live.

It is in turn humorous, serious, poignant, and wacko – just like life itself. It is not intended as an exposé of any sort. It does reveal, however, a lot of information about life that most people might take for granted, such as the training of school bus drivers, the resilience of school kids, and the impact of far-off events on all of us. Expect the unexpected.

Disclaimer: Memories can differ and memories can change. This memoir is the writer's personal recollection of events. The names of all students and their family members have been changed to protect their privacy.

Introduction:

A Crack in the Cosmic Egg

In the beginning of the year 2008, so early in the spring that the snow still covered the ground to a considerable extent, I decided to get a Commercial Driver's License. I thought a CDL would come in handy as the economy careened toward disaster like a dismasted schooner headed for the rockiest shore you could ever imagine.

I had been in real estate since 1980. I had begun my career in a baptism of fire during the early months of 1981 when the mortgage interest rate hovered between 19% and 21.5%. I'd witnessed the Wall Street Panic of 1986 and weathered numerous disastrous dips and meteoric rises in the market. And I had been watching throughout the two years of 2006 and 2007 as the market peaked and flattened.

During all of these times, I had been advised by the real estate gurus, the banks, the whole apparatus of the financial industry, that "this is the best time ever to buy; this is the best time ever to sell," with reasons appended to fit the current conditions. I had been here many times before; now here we were again. I knew very well what was about to happen. The market was about to jump off another cliff.

Now I was sixty-seven. My big account in Canada had suddenly imploded and gone belly-up; builders had stopped buying land to build 'spec' houses on; three men my age or younger with whom I'd worked died within the span of two months; my wife was planning to retire at the end of 2008; and I could see what was coming. It was time for me to retire.

As part of retirement, I thought it would be a good idea to get a Commercial Driver's License. I figured it would give me the ability to pick up odd driving jobs around town if I needed a little extra cash, which I suspected I might.

On March 11, 2008, Jim Cramer, an investment guru on CNBC's Mad Money program, said, responding to an inquiry, "Should I be worried about Bear Stearns in terms of liquidity and get my money out of there? No! No! No! Bear Stearns is fine! Do not take your money out...Bear Stearns is not in trouble. I mean, if anything, they're more likely to be taken over. Don't move your money from Bear! That's just being silly! Don't be silly!"

On March 17, 2008, Bear Stearns, which had very shortly before been selling at $133 a share, was sold to J P Morgan Chase for $2 a share. TV was most interesting that night, as the networks compared the marchers in the St. Patrick's Day Parade on New York's Fifth Avenue with fired Bear Stearns workers emerging from their offices a couple of blocks away carrying cardboard boxes full of their belongings and looking pretty, well, grim.

The next day, I called Bob Magee, the Director of Transportation at the Chittenden East Supervisory School District here in Vermont and asked him if he knew of any commercial driver training schools in the area. His response was a shocker. "You agree to give me two or three years of driving," Bob said, "and we'll train you for free."

So there it was. I had unwittingly hit upon one of the few professions that was hiring in this job market. Suddenly, strangely, right there in my lap was a job training program and a job if I wanted it; a local job at that, part-time both daily and yearly. It seemed pretty ideal as a retirement position. Not only did I get school holidays and vacations off, I got the whole summer off to do with as I pleased. And I didn't have to do lesson plans, either. Besides that, it seemed to be a tradition around here that when you retired, you drove a school bus. I was intrigued. I thought about it for a couple of hours.

I can't say I thought too deeply about it. I didn't know enough to think deeply about it. All I had were a few memories. I remembered Carl White, an IBM executive who retired at the time of the first-ever workforce cuts at that corporation. Carl picked up a job driving a school bus for the Essex School District.

"But I wasn't cut out for it," Carl said. "I kept confusing the tachometer and the speedometer. This was pointed out to me one day by a friendly officer who wondered why I was going fifty-five in a thirty-mile-per-hour zone. I explained to him that I wasn't going much over twenty. He explained to me how the court system was set up, and when to appear. I went back to golf."

I remembered my old high school buddy, Chuck McCurdy. He had moved down to South Carolina when he retired and also started driving as a retirement job. McCurdy had never been known for his mild and placid disposition. When I asked him how he dealt with rowdy behavior on the school bus, he said, "I just pull over to the side of the road and let them decide when they want to go home." Chuck had obviously mellowed.

This led to a memory of a story I was told about a Vermont driver back in the old days. "When we got out of hand," the former student told me, "Mr. Coulter—I don't think he had a first name—Mr. Coulter stopped the bus, got up, faced us with the veins in his neck bulging, and yelled 'Quiet, by jeesum!' We got quiet in a hurry, and stayed quiet."

Another whole series of memories arose, all of them centered around being stuck behind a school bus when I had to be somewhere in ten minutes and it would already take fifteen minutes to get there. The blasted school bus stops would add additional precious minutes to the journey. I would be even later than I was when I started out, the day would be ruined, and it would all be the fault of that blasted school bus. Not to mention what it was doing to my rising blood pressure and the volume of smoke coming out of my ears. "Know what I mean?" as one of my future riders would say.

But those cumulative scenes gave way to a different memory. This scene had occurred on a sunny afternoon in springtime when I was headed north on Pleasant Valley Road in Underhill. I was on my way to Jeffersonville, and for once I wasn't fighting the clock. I came up over a hill, and there was a school bus stopped in front of me. Its stop sign was sticking out, its red lights were flashing, and kids were hopping off of it. On the left was a meadow with a pond in it. Geese waddled along the edge of the pond, squawking. There was a slight breeze, and the trees swayed gently.

I took in this idyllic scene, and then I looked up at the back of the school bus. It was crammed with kids—kids in all manner, shape, and size. They were doing the things kids do—laughing, joking, turning around to wave at me. A couple of the guys wore baseball caps at jaunty angles and were talking a mile a minute. Arms flailed away in gestures all the way up and down the interior of the bus. A teenage boy and girl in the back seat were oblivious to the scene around them and looked *so* seriously into each other's eyes.

I followed that bus all the way up the valley. It must have made five more stops before it turned off onto a side road. But it didn't hold me up much, and I wouldn't have cared if it had. I was fascinated. By the kids. By their behavior. By their futures. Where were they going? Where was this bus taking them?

I held onto that scene for a long time. Something happened to me at that moment. It was like being with Dorothy in "The Wizard of Oz." Remember? When the farmhouse was caught in the tornado and it was flying through the air and then it crashed? And the door flew open? And the world outside turned Technicolor?

It was like watching a cosmic egg crack open. Out of the greyness and turmoil that the real estate world had become, there was a bright new world opening right before me, full of kids and their doings; full of early-morning rides and changing seasons. I didn't know the meaning of all those scenes flashing in front of my eyes. I didn't know what to expect. But boy, was I curious.

Before I went into real estate, I had taught for a good number of years. I knew kids. I knew what they could do. I figured I could handle them okay. My decision was made.

I called Bob Magee back and said, "When do I start?"

Bob explained that there were a number of things I had to do before I began driving. I needed to get scheduled for written and vision tests with the Department of Motor Vehicles. But first, I would have to attend a Bus Drivers Clinic certified by the State, because you couldn't take the tests without attending the clinic. There was one scheduled for April in Essex, and I signed up for it. Bob also suggested that I get started by reading the CDL laws and regulations. "Cover to cover, and memorize them," he said. He wasn't kidding.

I was really eager to get started. The next day, I went down to Motor Vehicles and got copies of the manuals. The Vermont Commercial Driver License Manual, I found, is 142 pages long. The Vermont School Bus Driver's Manual is 66 pages. They are both chock-full of interesting reading, and I don't mean easy, New York Times best-seller-fiction style reading, either. I mean really concentrated reading.

Not all of the Vermont Commercial Driver License Manual pertained to school buses. Some chapters were devoted solely to tractor trailers; some to transporting hazardous waste; some to tank vehicles; some to other combination types of vehicles: doubles, triples, that sort of thing. Triples!? But a huge amount of it was relevant to school buses and how to operate them. Enough material to choke a horse, as a matter of fact. And of course, the whole Vermont School Bus Driver's Manual was devoted entirely to the operation of school buses. There is an amazing swarm of facts and procedures contained within the covers of these manuals.

Here are just a few of the great store of facts I found on my way toward that fall semester of 2008:

> A school bus weighs 36,000 pounds.
>
> School buses are equipped with seven mirrors. Even with all that coverage, there is a blind spot behind the bus which can extend for as much as 400 feet.
>
> There are 480,000 school buses operating in the United States on any given school day.
>
> More students are killed getting on or off a school bus each year than are killed as passengers inside of a school bus. Extraordinary procedures are in effect to prevent deaths and injuries. These are strict procedures that must be followed constantly.
>
> You would not believe the variety of hazardous materials that are transported over the roads of America every day: fuel oils; lighter fluid; hair spray; charcoal; formaldehyde; asbestos; hydrochloric acid; battery acid; uranium; plutonium; pesticides; arsenic; hydrogen peroxide; ammonium nitrate; matches;

> fuses; gasoline fuel; acetone; propane; oxygen; helium; fireworks; ammunition; and dynamite. It's all out there waiting to get you. The only people standing between you and this stuff are trained, alert commercial drivers.
>
> Sleep is not voluntary. If you are drowsy, you can fall asleep and never even know it. Being drowsy, you are likely to have 'micro sleeps'—brief naps that last around four or five seconds. At 55 mph, that's a hundred yards. Guess what can happen in 100 yards.
>
> Alcohol management. There is no such thing. Your liver can only process about 1/3rd of an ounce of alcohol per hour, which means the rest of it is running around in your body, doing all kinds of interesting and sometimes really dangerous things to you, and in many instances, to others. For this reason, if a school bus driver is tested and found to have an alcohol level ¼ the legal limit, that driver is immediately removed from his or her duties and is subject to disciplinary action.

Those were just a few of the things I found out even before I started training. The actual amount of factual material you have to master is scary. Please bear with me a moment before we board that school bus. I'd like to share with you a list of requirements you need to fulfill to become a school bus driver in Vermont:

> You need to have a physical exam conducted by a licensed physician, physician's assistant, or nurse practitioner. The physician must submit to the State a Physical Examination Form which includes a Driver Eyesight Evaluation. (If you have high blood pressure,

you can get a three-month license, during which time you have to get the blood pressure under control. If you don't, you don't drive a school bus.)

You need to attend a school bus driver-training clinic (an eight-hour day designed for review for current school bus drivers and as initiation for new applicants, with the emphasis on safety and new rules and regs).

You need a valid commercial driver's license with a passenger endorsement and a school bus endorsement. In order to obtain that license, you need to pass state vision, written, and skills tests.

You must submit an official driver operating record covering the past three years.

You must have a background check involving several agencies including the FBI and Homeland Security.

You must go to the sheriff's office and be fingerprinted.

You must submit three letters of recommendation to the school district from your acquaintances, all of whom say to you "You're doing *what*?"

In the case of the Chittenden East Supervisory Union, you have to be interviewed by the Superintendent of Schools.

You must spend weeks being trained by the school's licensed school bus driver trainers, all the while being evaluated by them.

You are subject to an initial urinalysis and unannounced random urinalyses during the school year. Ultimately, you have to pass the dreaded **Road Test,** which includes the **Pre-Trip Inspection Test.**

All of these requirements are considered necessary to insure the safety and security of the students who will be in your charge; and in truth, if anything is ever a vital and valid concern, the safety of the kids is it. It really is, and as I walked and on occasion crawled through the qualification steps, I was extremely impressed by the seriousness with which everyone I met conducted the process. State examiners, clinic directors, school district administrators, the trainers, the mechanics, and the bus drivers themselves are all *very* serious people when it comes to making sure that a candidate is as well-prepared as absolutely possible. I cannot stress strongly enough the amount of attention to detail and concentration that goes into the seemingly simple task of getting a child from home to school and back home again in one piece, and in the process hopefully giving that student a decent sense of security.

So you don't just get into a school bus and tootle on down the road. And that's a good thing, because there's an awful lot to learn before you do, and a very precious cargo that you are going to be carrying.

But even with all the hoops there were to jump through and all the facts and skills there were to be learned – I couldn't wait to get started!

July, 2008

Training: Day One

Mt. Mansfield High School, Jericho, Vermont
Monday, July 7, 2008 - 10:30 AM

"Turn on the ignition," said Craig Moody.

I turned the key.

"Check all the gauges on the dash."

I looked at them. They all seemed to be indicating the expected values.

"Turn on the engine."

The big diesel roared. The bus shook.

"Put your foot on the brake."

"Right." I pressed down on the pedal.

"Release the emergency brake. Just press down hard on it."

I stared down at the emergency brake release.

"The big yellow button over there in the middle."

He didn't have to tell me that. I knew which one it was. I was just approaching it with caution. Finally, I did as instructed. The loud hiss of the adjusting air system filled the bus.

"Keep your foot on the brake. Put the gearshift into 'Drive' position."

I did.

"Check all your mirrors. Is everything clear around the bus?"

I checked. "As far as I can tell, yes."

"Good," Craig said. "Release the brake, and at the same time—very gently—press down on the accelerator."

"What?"

"Check the mirrors again," he said. "Foot off the brake, press the accelerator, point the bus down that driveway, and let's go for a ride." Craig was sitting in the frontmost seat on the right side of the bus, watching my every move.

"A ride?" I said.

"Sure," he said. I could swear he snickered. "Why not?"

I took a deep breath and pressed down on the accelerator. The 72-passenger yellow behemoth lurched forward, then settled into a nice, slow, maybe 5-mph speed headed down the driveway that led from the bus garage through the student parking lot and onto Brown's Trace Road. I liked that speed.

As we approached a combination speed bump/water bar set diagonally across the drive, we came to a sign that read: "All school buses must come to a complete stop." I stepped on the brake. The bus slammed to a halt.

"Easy. Easy," Craig said. "Don't forget, you have to press on that brake real easy. Don't worry, you'll get used to it. Let's go."

I stepped on the accelerator again. Gingerly. The big bus rocked back and forth gently once, then twice, as the front wheels passed over the hump. I breathed easier, and sped up. Suddenly the rear of the bus lifted violently as the back wheels went up over the bar and crashed down onto the pavement again. "Good God!" I said.

"Don't let go of the wheel," Craig said quietly. "Okay, you're coming up to another stop sign. Brake gently, now. Good. That's better. Much smoother."

The third stop sign was at Brown's Trace Road. Before I pulled out, I stopped and turned on the right-hand turn signal. "Good," said Craig. "Now, before you go, listen. When you're turning one of these babies, what you want to do is take all the road you can before you begin to turn. I mean, of course, all of your side of the road. But you want to get it out there, otherwise, when you turn, your rear wheels will end up in the ditch, the bus will rock back and forth like it did up there at the speed bump, and everyone will get excited and nervous, and you don't want that. You are the authority here, and if you're putting this thing into a ditch, they'll lose faith in you. And everybody, you included, will have a bad day. Okay, check to see nothing's coming, and pull out."

I drove smoothly and cleanly onto Brown's Trace. "Hey, that was good!" Craig said. "Now, bring it up to the speed limit. What's the speed limit here?"

"Thirty-five," I said, as the big bus surged forward.

"Good," said Craig. "You saw the 35-mph sign. Don't ever forget to read the traffic signs. Get up to speed—by that, I mean the speed limit—and don't exceed it. Ever. Remember what the manual says: the safest speed is the speed that the majority of traffic is going, up to the speed limit. I cannot emphasize that enough. You must not go over the speed limit. Know why?"

"Because it's against the law?"

"Well, yeah, that's a good reason. And here's another good reason: if a school bus driver is caught doing 15 miles over the limit, that's an automatic yank of his license. Sort of cuts off access to your salary. But the third reason is this: somebody will report you. Honest to God. Somebody is always watching you. And they report you. They report us for anything. Hitting a curb. Taking a turn too sharp. Stopping too fast. Being where they think we're not supposed to be. They'll pick up their cell phone while they're following you and call up the school or the troopers or the newspapers or whatever else they feel like calling and report you. Let me tell you a story: an irate citizen called Bob up from Arlington one day to report one of our buses speeding along at about twenty miles over the limit.

Bus 28, it was. Arlington! That's about a hundred miles south of here, ain't it? More, maybe. So Bob checked everything out. Checked to see if Bus 28 was on a field trip. Found out it was parked about a hundred feet away from his office. Make a long story short, that informer was looking at our new Bus 28, which was being delivered north from the bus manufacturer in North Carolina. The manufacturer had already put all our decals and letters on it: Chittenden East Supervisory District. Home Of The Cougars. Bus 28.

So here comes the new bus, rippin' north as fast as the driver can get it to go, which is 65, because it's on a governor and the manufacturer won't let it go over 65 for the first thousand miles, and it's in a 55-mph speed zone, and here comes our informer, and he's right about the bus and the ID, but it ain't ours yet. But he isn't takin' no for an answer, and... what's your speed?"

I looked down at the speedometer, and as I was about to report 34 mph, I looked up. I was headed off the road. I hit the gravel, grabbed the steering wheel tight, and wrestled the bus back onto the asphalt. Slowly. Deliberately. I'd gone about a foot onto the shoulder. I couldn't believe it.

"Watch the road," said Craig. His voice was serious. "Good. You're back."

I let out my breath.

"That's why a bus driver is not supposed to talk to anyone while he's driving the bus," said Craig. "There's so much to watch, you just gotta leave the chatter alone. Unless some kid's screamin' that there's blood all over the place. Hey, we're coming up to the intersection. Remember what I told you about your turn. You're gonna turn right."

Brown's Trace ends at a T with Route 15, a heavily traveled road. There was traffic coming from the left and the right. Lots of it. Finally I saw an opportunity. I pulled out, turning right. But I didn't pull out far enough. True to Craig's warning, the back right tires ended up in the gravel on the apron. The bus lurched and whomped and righted itself and proceeded east on Route 15. I am not kidding when I say the bus did all that. It did. I didn't. I don't know exactly what I was doing at that point, but there we were, heading east on Route 15, the Grand Army of the Republic Highway.

"Told ya," said Craig. "Next, we're gonna turn right onto Pleasant Valley Road."

There's a half-mile-long stretch on Route 15 between Brown's Trace and Pleasant Valley Road, and all of a sudden I had the bus up to 50 mph, the stated speed limit. And it felt good. It felt right. I passed a semi heading in the opposite direction. The driver nodded to me, and I nodded back. A recognition. Kings of the road. All of a sudden I realized that I'd looked directly into the eyes of that semi driver. I was on the same level with him. I mean, I wasn't as experienced as he was, or as knowledgeable, or as skilled. It was just that I was at the same height as he was. The same height.

When I'd climbed up into that driver's seat, I never even thought about that, but a school bus is a really big vehicle. It's 40 feet long and 8 feet wide, and anywhere from 10 to 11.5 feet high. You sit as high as a semi driver, which means that your eyes are about 7 ½ feet off the ground. Right then I felt this was really cool. I could see forever, all over the place, and that was a very cool thing, and a very safe thing, as well. You can see what's comin' atcha' and prepare for it, and be ready to dismantle whatever disaster is headed your way long before it gets to you. Of course, you can't be prepared for everything, but you can try hard, and when you come right down to it, that's what this training is all about: Safety.

This trip may sound like I'd been stuck in the driver's seat cold turkey for my first day of Bus Driver's Ed, but that wasn't really the case. Before taking it out, Craig and I had inspected that vehicle top to bottom, even to crawling under it. He showed me every piece of equipment on that bus. He stressed safety and care. He told me about the checkpoint program that our head mechanic, Earl, had instituted. Earl kept a running account of everything that happened to every bus, down to each ding, the date it was acquired, and who acquired it.

"Report any defect to Earl immediately," Craig told me. "Anything you think is wrong mechanically. If you happen to scrape by some bushes hanging out in the road, report it. If you don't, Earl will spot the damage at some point. He has very keen eyes. There is no escape."

Craig paused and smiled, a wicked gleam in his eye. "You will inspect the bus every morning," he continued. "That's part of your job description. Make sure everything is in perfect working order. Check all the fluid levels. If you run out of oil and ruin an engine, you won't have to worry about getting fired, though, because Earl will probably kill you before Bob gets a chance to fire you."

When we returned from our run through Underhill, Craig handed me a five-page checklist and said, "This is what we'll be doing for the next couple of weeks, until you get to doing it right. You'll have to know each part of the bus, what it looks like, what it does, what it does when it isn't working right, and how to test for that. We'll do that every morning, then we'll go out for a ride and practice turning, backing, left and right backing turns, crossing railroads, city driving, Interstate driving, backroads driving, picking up passengers, dropping them off, loop-de-loops, everything you'll need to know. About the only thing we won't do is winter driving. Unless it snows this summer."

And that's what we did. Every night I studied that checklist. Every morning we did a total inspection of that bus. Every night I went home and studied what I had missed that day. Then we would do it again the next day, and I would forget different things each day, and I would go home and try to remember them in different ways, using different mind tricks. I found I had to dig deep, way back into my memory bank, all the way back to working on 1953 Chevys and MGs. There was valuable information stored there. I actually had replaced a couple of head gaskets back then. I had helped to take apart engines and ream out the piston holes and replace crankshafts—all ancient crafts in this age, but still valuable. I hadn't done anything like that since 1962, but the memories were still there. I couldn't understand how anybody who had never done anything like that could remember all this stuff, but evidently they could, because they did, and they passed their tests, and so did I.

But it wasn't easy. I had a particularly hard time getting down the difference between an air canister, an air dryer, and an air tank. And you would be surprised at how easy it can be to forget what to call U-bolts until you nickname them U-boats. But finally, one day as I had my head way down deep in the engine compartment, calling out components and what to look for and why, Earl dropped by to check some papers out with Craig. I stopped reeling out facts and figures and Earl said, "No. No. Keep going." So I did, until I had finished with everything stored under the hood and also anywhere else upon the earth. Earl spoke with Craig about whatever was on that paper and then left. Later, Craig told me Earl had been impressed with my recitation, and that it wasn't easy to impress Earl. That made me feel good.

It took a couple of weeks to get to that stage, though. And it was hot. Tiring. I was beginning to wonder if I would ever get the whole thing down right. For instance, one morning after crawling around under the bus and inspecting the entire exterior, we finally got inside and Craig had me go through the functions of the gauges and switches and other miscellaneous stuff like the horn location, and I just could not satisfy him. He would just sit there and say, after I went through everything, "Nope. You missed something. Go through it again." And I would, and he'd say again, "Nope. Missed something. Do it again. Got to make sure of everything before you start each morning." And I'd do it again, and he'd shake his head again, negative. I just couldn't get it right. Finally, I turned toward him and said. "Oh, come on, Craig. Tell me. I can't figure it out."

Smooth as silk, Craig said, "Look at the hood."

"The hood?" I wheeled around to look at the hood. "What's wrong with the h...?"

It was open. It was staring at me like some great yellow shark surging up out of the asphalt, heading right for me with its jaws open and evil on its mind. I had been so intent on getting the gauges and switches right that I hadn't even looked out the windshield. I hadn't even noticed that I didn't close the hood after inspecting the engine compartment.

"You know," said Craig, "You do that at the road test, you'd probably flunk it unless the examiner died of a heart attack from laughing too much."

Ah, yes. Training was a humbling experience. But at last, Craig pronounced me ready. He cut the lessons down to a couple per week, just to keep me tuned up, and we waited for the big day of the Road Test.

On the morning of August 5th, Craig took me out for one last spin. He'd washed the bus inside and out that morning and it looked grand and gleaming in the August sun. We drove over roads I'd driven many times before. During the past few weeks, I had spent a lot of time on back gravel roads, on two-lane country roads, on the Interstate, and in the grand metropolis of Burlington. Everywhere we went, Craig took the opportunity to find railroad tracks for me to cross. He had me backing up and turning on gravel roads with no shoulders. He placed cones out in parking lots and had me put that bus backwards through them, left reverse turns and right reverse turns. He had me perform every twist and turn that bus was capable of until he was satisfied that I knew something about how to handle it. He didn't ask me to do loop-de-loops, but I expected that to happen any day.

Now here we were on the big day. I drove into the inspection station and parked. Craig got out. I followed, placing the chocks under the rear wheels. Craig introduced me to the examiner and promptly disappeared.

Well, I passed the test. Think I did pretty well with it too. At least that's what the examiner told me—that I had a good, solid test result. I got under the hood and rattled off the parts, what they did, and what problems to look for. I got under the bus and yelled out to him what was there and what problems to look for. I proved I knew the difference between an air canister, an air dryer, an air compressor, and an air tank. I did the air brake test correctly. I started up the engine using the correct procedures. I even remembered to remove the chocks from the wheels before beginning the driving part of the test.

I didn't go over any center islands when I turned. I didn't exceed any speed limits. When it was time to pull to the side of the road for the scheduled emergency stop, I did the procedure correctly. While we were sitting there, the examiner pointed to a nearby cliff and told me that he saw a big buck up on top of it almost every day. I glanced at the cliff and then immediately back at the road. I have never been able to figure out if that examiner was just being cordial or if he wanted to see if I would fixate on that cliff and try to see a buck. Well, if he wanted the latter, he didn't get it. But I knew what he really wanted. He wanted to see my eye movements. Examiners look for an applicant to constantly look around, at an average of twelve eye movements per minute. I didn't disappoint him there.

I didn't disappoint him at the railroad crossing, either. Just as I finished explaining my routine before crossing the tracks, the gates went down and a train came through. So I got to do that twice. All twenty-four steps. Got it right, too. Twice.

I even remembered to put the hood down before starting on the exam run, thus saving the examiner from a premature death by laughter.

At the end of that exam, I was a full-fledged school bus driver. I went home and spent the rest of that sunny afternoon puttering around the yard, looking at everything I had to do to get it in shape. But I didn't do a thing. I had done enough for one day.

August, 2008

The Shortest Month

August is a lush month in the hills that make up the western slopes of the Green Mountains of Vermont.

On a good day in August, the farmers and gardeners can feel their crops grow. The mountain streams sparkle. In those streams, the brook trout lie hidden under submerged rocky outcroppings, disturbed only by an occasional fisherman. The fisher might be human or bear or otter or fisher cat. Foxes and coyotes roam the grown-over fields left fallow since the nineteenth century. Barred owls hoot like crazy in the middle of the summer night. Moose thunk along the mountain byways in the evening, and deer are everywhere. There is a lot of wild country back up in those hills. Innumerable critters roam around up there beyond where the old mountain roads end. There's a good reason that teams from Mt. Mansfield High School are known as the Cougars.

The Chittenden East Supervisory Union towns—Huntington, Richmond, Jericho, Bolton, and Underhill—ramble along the western flanks of Mt. Mansfield and Camel's Hump. Mt. Mansfield is the highest mountain in Vermont, and Camel's Hump, just to the south, is not far behind. These two mountains, with innumerable lesser peaks, make up a good part of the main spine of the Green Mountains stretching up the middle of the state from Bennington in the south to Derby Line in the north. The Long Trail winds and pitches across their summits and is easily accessible from any number of branch trails along its length.

Residents of the towns can at times simply walk out their back doors and head up into the forests on old woods roads that eventually turn into trails. They can follow these trails, or for that matter, streams, up into places like Nebraska Notch, or Preston Ponds, or dozens of other beautiful backcountry spots. If they've a mind to, these lucky people of the mountain towns can ramble up and over the heights and down the other side into Stowe and the Mad River Valley and come back the same day. But mostly they are content to get to the top and wander around up there. People generally reserve the over-the-hill trips for winter, when they strap on snowshoes and pack a pair of skis on their backs and travel up and down on one or the other of these, depending on the terrain and the snow conditions.

These towns, like a lot of others in Vermont, have been blessed with forests and wild places and farms still operating. But it's not all life in the woods here. There's a lot more going on. For work, there's IBM in Essex, and the Medical Center and the University of Vermont and Champlain College and Burlington College in Burlington, and St. Michael's College in Colchester, and the National Guard, and NRG and all the other start-up alternative energy companies in towns all over the county, so there's a good base for employment, even in these precarious times. In our towns, we have farmers and woodsmen and engineers and PhDs and doctors and artists and sculptors. We tend to drive Subarus and Ford pick-ups and the like, and our houses (the ones you can see from the main roads, anyway) are generally modest by current standards.

Politically, we have the usual mix. The spectrum goes from far left to far right. As with the rest of the state, we tend to respect each other's positions and speak politely to one another. There's an excellent reason for this cautious approach to politics, beside it being the polite thing to do. Because there are so few of us, we never know when some looming issue will unite or divide us. Your enemy of today may be your greatest ally of tomorrow. That keeps us civil. In this respect, small is beautiful. Knowing your neighbors on an individual basis, and understanding their political and religious positions and respecting them, and leaving them alone when they want to be alone, and extending a hand to them when they need some help: that's what you do, because that's what they're doing for you, too. When the sun sets over these small mountain communities, people settle in, and are fairly content, except for the usual worries over money, health, taxes, the state of the union, global warming, the origin of the universe, and what the kids are going to get into next. In short, the same worries that have afflicted the race ever since it knew it was a race, no matter what town or country it happened to live in.

In effect, this particular August, pinched between my August 5th road test and the Drivers Meeting called by Bob Magee on the 25th, was twenty days long—days that I appreciated tremendously. There wasn't much to do as far as business was concerned, except fingerprinting at the sheriff's office, and filling out and delivering forms to the Supervisory District office, and meeting with the Superintendent of Schools. Superintendent James Massingham and I had an affable meeting at his office, during which time I assume he ascertained that I was probably not a threat to the school system, since at the end of the meeting he and I signed a contract for the school year 2008-2009, and I officially joined the CESU district staff.

The August 25th Drivers Meeting was held in the bus garage at Mount Mansfield High School. The buses were backed out, the tools were pushed against the walls, the floor was washed, and the place was impeccably clean. The mechanics and trainers brought in 2 x 8 folding tables and chairs and placed them in a U-formation. The meeting began after the drivers had a light breakfast and all the coffee they could stand. Bob opened by asking all the drivers to introduce themselves and state the number of years they had been driving. I was amazed. Some of these veterans had been driving twenty, thirty years. I introduced myself, stated my experience as zero years, and received a hearty round of applause—a greeting, I supposed, designed to hearten the rookie as he stepped into the unknown.

Not all of the drivers had twenty or thirty year credentials. Some had only fifteen, or eight, or six years. Most of them, like myself, had stepped into their positions from other vocations. There were retired IBM engineers, women who left higher-paying positions so they could be closer to their kids while they were going through school, an ex-pilot or two, a swordsmith, a farmer (who still farmed), construction workers, small entrepreneurs—all people who had paid their dues. There were 12 women and 24 men.

They were led by Bob Magee, who had come to the Chittenden East district fourteen years before, from another Vermont district that had decided to change from a district-owned fleet to a private bus fleet. Bob didn't like that, and as much as he liked the old district, he decided to make a move. It wasn't an easy decision. He had grown up in that part of the state, K through 12. After high school, he had joined the Guard; and when he came home, he was hired as a bus driver. He couldn't understand why. He had been pretty much of a hell-raiser when he was a student. The transportation director explained that to him.

"He told me," says Bob wryly, "that I had been so much trouble on the bus for all those years, I must know everything that any trouble-maker could ever come up with, and be able to put a stop to it right away." Bob was able to do that, and he rose through the ranks to become the transportation director there.

When Bob came to Chittenden East, our district was experiencing a spate of vandalism. It was replacing 400 ripped, punctured, and otherwise vandalized bus seats per year. Bob put a stop to that. The figure now is 40 per year. Not bad for a fleet of 44 buses.

Bob knew how to deal with bad behavior. He began implementing systems to stop it in its tracks. On the interior front of every Chittenden East bus, and over the back door, too, there is a list of ten rules. If a student disregards any of the rules, he or she is liable to be written up by the driver. The writing up is done in quadruplicate, and copies go to Bob, to the principal of the school the student attends, to the guidance counselor in that school, and to the parents of the student. *Everybody* is in the loop. The student will pay a penalty for misbehavior. That penalty can be a meeting with the principal, a call from the school to the parents, a meeting of the parents and the principal and counselor, and on up. If the behavior does not improve, harsher penalties can be incurred. Three strikes and you're out, kid. If a student is written up three times, he can be kicked off the bus, and lose bus privileges for an entire year. This does not sit well with parents, who then have to get the kid to school and pick him up. It kind of gets parents upset. It kind of cuts down on misbehavior, too.

I have known a good number of executives, administrators, and supervisors. I have known excellent ones and absolutely terrible ones. I would place Bob Magee right at the top of the heap. He is tough but fair. He acts diligently. He protects his workers. He pays attention to detail. He is politically astute. He acts, and when he does, things happen fast. And he acts rationally, which a lot of administrators don't know how to do.

But back to the drivers' meeting, which lasted from 8 AM to 2 PM. First, as I said, there was coffee and breakfast. Then Bob opened the meeting. Cindy advised us on how to clean a bus, and reminded us that we were obliged to clean the buses every two weeks, inside and out. Leah distributed our route schedules based on the last year, and told us to bring in revisions after two weeks. Earl emphasized the need to keep on top of the condition of the buses and to report anything wrong mechanically, even if we thought it was nothing. An industrial psychologist gave us a talk on preparing for change, because there would be many changes coming up this year.

The economy was down. Bob was being pressed to economize, the same as all the departments of the district were. As a result, drivers for the most part would no longer deliver athletic teams to their 'away' games and pick them up at the end. Rather, they would deliver them and let the parents pick them up at wherever the games were played. This would cut the hours of some drivers significantly. This was only one of many changes to be dealt with during the coming year.

We had our pictures taken for our ID tags. Holly—the office manager/bookkeeper/substitute driver—wanted to know who needed new jackets and caps. Bob reviewed the paperwork needed to keep the department running smoothly. We covered the School Bus Vehicle Pre-Trip Inspection Report; the Bus Conduct Report; the Master Route Schedule; the Bus Washing Form; the Bus Washing Instructions; the CESU School Year Calendar; the Payroll Date Schedule; the Bi-Weekly Payroll Record; the list of Drivers and Contact Numbers form; the School Bus Expectations and Consequences for Violations Form; the Bus Seating Chart for Use in Accidents or Incidents; the Vermont State Police Statement Form for reporting an identifiable vehicle passing a stopped school bus illegally; the State Police Statement form for use in accident situations; the Vandalism Report; the instructions on Revising Your Route; the CESU Leave form; the sample school bus passes; the insurance forms; the contract forms; the Evaluation Form; and the Idling Policy and Guidelines.

And Bob gave us this warning: "Whatever you do," said Bob, "do not idle on school property when you're picking up or dropping off the kids. Don't forget who wrote that Bus Idling law. Brown's River Middle School wrote that law, delivered it to the legislature, and had it passed. *Especially* don't idle over there at Brown's River. They've already told me they'll be watching. Carefully. And they will be, too. You can bet on it."

It was a good law, that idling law, and it's been cutting back on a lot of pollution since it went into effect statewide. It was the kids from Brown's River Middle School who came up with it, along with their teacher, Patti Brushett.

After the meeting, we had lunch. The next day would be the first driving day. As a sort of dry run, we would pick up the new Mt. Mansfield freshmen and deliver them to the high school for orientation. Bob dismissed us, told us to check out our buses, and wished us good luck in the coming year. I drove home, not exactly *tingling* with excitement, but I *was* excited. I wouldn't have any trouble waking up early the next morning.

September, 2008

As we know,
There are known knowns.
These are things we know we know.
We also know
There are known unknowns.
That is to say,
We know there are some things
We do not know.
But there are also unknown unknowns,
The ones we don't know
We don't know.

D.K. Rumsfeld
Department of Defense news briefing
Feb 12, 2002

This was a month full of unknown unknowns, both for me and for the nation as a whole. As for me, I had the knowledge gained from the years before my real estate days when, in my other career as an educator, I had taught every grade from third through graduate school. That is, I had learned a lot about human behavior. I knew some of the things students would do. I had seen them before. These were the things I knew I knew.

But there were also known unknowns. I had never driven a school bus before, and I didn't know how students would act on a bus. The only student buses I had knowledge of were from long ago, from elementary school, when at the end of the school year, we got to drive up from Long Island to Rye Playland for the day. The overriding memory of those rides was the constant din of a bus full of kids singing "One Hundred Bottles of Beer on The Wall." The rendition was designed to kill time and drive the chaperones and drivers crazy. Singing that song was like telling the world to...well, telling the world that we were coming and we were going to mess it around somewhat even before we were teenagers. Typical early-middle-school behavior. High spirits out on an adventure. I didn't think that scenario would apply here. This was different: a daily routine, not an adventure. Little did I remember that any day was an adventure for at least some kids in any given situation.

As for the nation, its major known unknown was the outcome of the presidential race. But unknown unknowns lurk around every corner, as we shall shortly see. So it...

"WWWWWWAAAAAAAAHHHHH!!!!!!!!" Erin screamed as the bus door opened to let her off in front of her house on the afternoon of the first day of school.

Her mother stood there, her benign "welcome home, darling" smile changing to a mask of horror.

"WWWWWAAAAAAAAHHHHHHH!!!!!" the kindergartner screamed as she leapt into her mother's arms. I sat in the front right-hand seat of the bus, frozen. Alan was driving.

"First day willies," Alan growled to the mother. "She'll get over it. Good afternoon, Ma'am," he said, and matter-of-factly closed the bus doors. We went on.

If Craig had done the instruction, Alan was doing the practicum, teaching me what really happened when you drove. I had been a bit disappointed to find out that Alan was assigned to drive with me the first week. I thought I knew everything. I found out I didn't know anything.

"WWWWWAAAAAAAAAAHHHHHH!!!!!" went Ashley the next day. Ashley was Erin's next-door neighbor and kindergarten mate. I don't know if she was trying to imitate Erin or commiserate with her, or if something drastic had happened to this one. All I knew was that I was glad Alan was driving again.

"Second day willies," he muttered to Ashley's mother through his beard. "She'll get over it." Then he said to me over his shoulder, "Kindy-gartners." That's all he said, and all he needed to say. That one word told me what to expect from kindy-gartners in stress situations. Alan didn't tell me what to expect from them in non-stress situations, but that wasn't his job. His job was getting me off on the right foot, and he could do that without too many words.

Alan taught me how to find kids in the early morning mist. "Gotta look sharp," he said in his gravelly voice. "Never know where they're gonna pop up. Changes every day. Gotta be alert all the time, otherwise you'll miss them."

He taught me about dropping them off in the afternoon. That first afternoon run, he shouted, "Hey, any you kids know where people live? Come on up here!" Three fifth-grade girls—Nicole, Morgan, and Paige—popped up from the back and took seats behind Alan. They seemed to know where everybody lived and were more than happy to direct traffic. Fifth grade girls, I learned as the year went by, have the capacity to change from hysterical two-year-olds to mature, responsible thirty-year-olds in the space of a second or two. These three, for the moment at least, were pushing thirty-five and enjoying it.

It was important for me to note the difference between reading mailbox numbers off a sheet of paper and seeing these drop-off points where the kids actually lived in real life. While Alan drove and the girls directed, I sat and wrote furiously, trying to connect kids' names with their stops. I figured that the better I knew their names, the better I'd be able to talk with them. This is not as easy as it seems, as any teacher will tell you. You tend to learn the names of the trouble-makers first; then the characters; then the smart ones; then the rest sort of fill in over time, so that by April or May you have them all pretty much down. But my goal was to get their names down as quickly as possible. I wanted to greet them by name as they got on the bus every morning. I thought it would aid in encouraging some kind of order during the ride.

I think I was right about that, but my project had its ups and downs. Except in home room, a teacher doesn't normally call on every student every day; at least they didn't when I taught. Of course, classes are smaller now, so maybe they do. At any rate, as the days went on, I learned the names, but some days I would forget the ones I knew, and remembered new ones, and there were days when I would be reminded—sometimes forcefully—that I hadn't gotten it right. One morning I greeted a little kindy-gartner out on the furthest loop of the route with a smile.

"Good morning, Maria!"

"Don't call me that!" she snarled. "I'm not Maria. I'm Mariah!"

And she strode off down the aisle in high dudgeon. Oops. Sorrrry.

Sometimes I didn't need to learn their names. On the first day, at a stop where five kids got on with two sets of parents standing there to see them off, another little kindy-gartner hopped onto the first step, turned to face his folks, waved to the assembled multitude, and announced: "Farewell!"

He waved again with a gesture as practiced as any politician's, turned, hopped up the rest of the way into the bus, and took a seat. He was immediately christened "Little Dude" by the gaggle of fifth-grade girls. They said he was cute.

They thought "Purple Backpack Dude" was cute, too. "Purple Backpack Dude" was an eighth grader who, in typical eighth-grade fashion, didn't pay any attention to fifth graders but purposefully stormed to the back of the bus and joined his peers in joyful disdain of anything on the bus that wasn't an eighth grader. But the fifth-grade girls didn't care how he acted. They had him pegged. He was "Purple Backpack Dude" from that day on. I didn't know until February that his name was Hunter, which I thought was pretty cool all by itself.

But obviously the fifth-grade girls were culture carriers, and they held a lot of sway in determining the social order on the bus. To some extent they were forced into this, because this was their first year in middle school. They were lowest on the totem pole there, where the year before they were on the highest social rung of the elementary school herd—the social elite, as it were. They had to be a force now or be ground to bits. So they were cohesive, and formed a kind of bridge between the elementary and middle school ranks.

The high school students were a different story entirely. They were mature. The true elite. They were so far above the eighth graders and all the rest of them that they didn't even bother to disdain them. They just pretended they didn't exist. There were only a few high schoolers, but I could always count on them to establish a veneer of civilization and sophistication on the bus. I'm not kidding. Whenever one of them got on, they trailed a sort of aura about them. They were different. They were almost grown-ups, and the little kids (well, not the real little ones, but the little ones down to where they began realizing there were beings in the world other than themselves) looked at them with awe.

So there it was: I had a veritable one-room schoolhouse and homeroom combined. I had everyone from Pleasant Valley on that bus from kindergarten to twelfth grade. And anything could go wrong with any of them at any time, a situation that should instill an immense sense of terror in any adult.

Alan went on giving me pointers all that first week. One thing he was especially insistent about was the care that had to be taken getting the kids on the bus and letting them off. Picking up and dropping off on the right side of the street was a lot easier than on the left, where they had to cross the street.

Let's look at the left side pickup: start the ambers, brake, come to a stop while watching to see that the traffic coming toward you is also stopped in both directions. Look in all the mirrors. Crack the door so the reds go on. Look for any traffic

again. Look at the kids waiting for the bus. Make sure they're watching you. Look for moving traffic again. Clear? Okay, give the kids the thumbs-up to cross. Make sure they look both ways before they start. Follow them as they cross and board the bus. Say good morning to them as they pass you. Wait until they sit down. All this time, watch for traffic. Okay. Got 'em.

Disembarking: brake, get the ambers on, stop, crack the door to activate the reds. Watch that the traffic is stopped. The kids get up. Look for any dangerous situation. All the vehicles stopped? Okay, let them out, but be sure to tell them if there's ice on the road. Count them as they get off. Make a note of the number. Make sure they all exit okay, that they walk along the side of the road to a place ten feet ahead of the bus, that they stop, that they're looking at you. Check the traffic again. Okay? Count them again. Give them the thumbs-up. Watch them cross the road. When they get to the other side, out of the right-of-way and you know they're safe, count them again. Make sure it's the same number that left the bus. Only then can you deactivate the reds and move on.

It drove Alan nuts when some of the kids didn't follow this plan that first week. Most of them did. When they were leaving the bus, Alan would instruct them, "Wait for my thumbs-up." Finally, one morning toward the end of the week, when we were coming to the end of a run, Alan pulled the bus over to the side of the road, put the four-way flashers on, waited for silence (which wasn't long in coming; the kids were curious about what he was about to do to them) and announced loudly, "You don't wait for my thumbs-up, I'm gonna write you up!"

Magic words. "Write you up." More trouble than it was worth, getting written up for such a stupid small infraction. A sense of impending trouble pervaded the bus. "Got it?" Alan said. They got it, all right. "And get your feet out of the aisle. Keep your feet out of the aisle. It's dangerous." Nods all over. Legs and arms disappeared from the aisle. Everyone faced front.

As we were letting the kids off at the elementary school before going on to the middle school, Alan said to me, "Keep after them until they wait for the thumbs-up. They know they're supposed to wait. If they don't wait, write 'em up. Might save a life somewhere down the line."

The thumbs-up signal was in effect all over the district. The kids got used to looking for it. Every driver used it, so when kids got mixed together for field trips or athletics, everybody was always looking for the same thing, the same routine. It was a good practice.

So was keeping all those arms and legs out of the aisle, although it was difficult, especially with the younger ones. There was just a natural urge to turn to your neighbor across the aisle and chat and exchange news and show off stuff you were bringing into school that day. Then all of a sudden the aisle could be full of talking heads and flailing arms, and if the bus for any reason hit anything (God forbid) there could be a lot of human damage. School buses are designed to contain the kids in their seats if there's an emergency stop, but it doesn't work if they're partway out of them.

It's hard on the kids, though. It's human nature to want to talk with your friends. It's especially hard if you're so small that you can't see over the seat, and there are all those kids around you wanting to talk, too, to tell you what happened last night, or in the cafeteria, or in science class, or whatever. I found out first-hand what it was like much later on in the year, when I scrunched down in a seat to the eye level of a first grader. It was freaky. I felt like I was in isolation. I wanted to reach out and yell "Hey! Anybody here?"

Toward the end of Week One, Alan let me drive. Then one afternoon he waved good-bye at the end of the run and said I was ready. I was on my own.

That's when the big September story began.

I was driving Bus 4 because of a set of circumstances I could not have envisioned when I began this journey.

As I was traveling through life, making decisions that would lead me to join Bob Magee's team, other things were occurring. The most important circumstance, and the most tragic, was that Phil Halsey died. Phil had driven Bus 4 for years. The kids knew and loved him. Phil came home from the last trip of the 2007-2008 school year, complained of a headache, collapsed, and died in his wife's arms, even before any first responders could get there.

Phil lived right down in the middle of Underhill Center, in a big old rambling white farmhouse. He was retired, but was active in town on a number of committees and public initiatives. He was a quiet-spoken gentleman of the old school, more interested in cooperation than confrontation. He was a problem-solver.

Everybody loved Phil. There was no way I could replace him.

But Bob Magee asked me to drive Phil's route, because I lived right up the hill above Underhill Center. A tradition had grown up that Bus 4 was left for the school year in the commuter lot next to the old Center School down the street from Phil's place. (Leaving the bus there instead of bringing it to the bus garage every night saved two gallons of fuel per day. Multiply that by 180 days, and then again by $3.00 per gallon of diesel fuel, and you will find that parking #4 in the Center saved the District well over $1000 a year in fuel costs.) So Phil had actually walked to work.

I wasn't about to do that—it was a mile-and-a-half from my house. That doesn't sound bad until you figure in an elevation change of a few hundred feet and throw in a couple of feet of snow to boot, but heck, it's an easy drive. A great commute. Probably the best commute in the world. So it was a natural that I would take over for Phil.

The great majority of kids had heard about Phil's death back in June. That didn't mean they were over it. The ones who hadn't heard were shocked; the ones who had were in mourning. Think of it. A reliable factor in your young life—one that's in place every morning and night—suddenly gone. Without warning. Even when a family breaks apart, there are usually warnings. When grandparents die, well, they are old. When other relatives die, very often there is some time to get prepared. But this is different. It may be part of the outside world, but it's a part on which you have relied for your entire school life. Stuff like this isn't supposed to happen. Bus drivers retire, move on, take other jobs. But they generally don't just die. They generally don't just leave a big hole in your reality.

But Phil was dead. There was this other unknown guy driving the bus. It was unsettling.

So, I thought of something. I thought of a lot of things, actually, trying to speed up the future. To change the air of sadness; to try to bring these kids back to an even keel; to give them a sense of continuity, of ownership, I decided to—sounds silly, but this is what I decided—I decided to have a contest.

One Friday morning in the middle of the month, when I reached Underhill Central School, a point in the route when everybody who was going to ride the bus was on the bus, I stood up and said, "Okay, everybody, listen up. This bus needs a name. On Monday, we will have an election to determine what we are going to name it. Think about it. We can talk more about it this afternoon. Hold your questions until then."

Oh, right. Hold your questions. After the barrage of questions, I said, "I'll have some answers for you this afternoon." Then I let the elementary students out, and we proceeded on to the Middle School where I would drop everybody else—the middle schoolers debarking; the high schoolers transferring to another bus that took them to Mount Mansfield Union H.S.

In the afternoon, I answered questions. Over the weekend, the students were to think about a name for the bus. On Monday afternoon, I would distribute secret ballots. Each student would write the name of their choice on a piece of paper, fold it over, and deliver it to me on their way off of the bus. If no one got a majority vote, there would be a run-off vote. However it went, we would have a name for the bus.

I did this with the kids on the Jericho afternoon run, too.

The kids jumped on it. They really liked it. They were excited. I was happy with that.

On Monday afternoon, I distributed ballots at the middle school. The kids got busy filling them out. When we got to the elementary schools, I distributed ballots to the kids as they filed past me. The middle schoolers were waiting for the smaller students as they made their way down the aisle. Cries came from the back of the bus: "What is this?" "Don't worry about what it is, just write what I tell you." "I can't write yet!" "Here, I'll write it for you. Just fold it over and hand it in."

It sounded like Tammany Hall back there. It sounded like a Chicago ward. I got up and looked over the disheveled, swaying mass of students. "Hey!" I yelled. "It's a *secret* ballot!"

"Don't worry!" came back a voice. "We're just helpin' 'em."

Well, actually, it went pretty well. The ballots got filled out quickly. Everyone took their seats. As the kids disembarked, they handed in their ballots, and I tucked them into my shirt pocket. I couldn't wait to see what they had come up with.

I had two runs in the afternoon. After dropping off the elementary and middle school students, I looped around to Underhill Central School again to wait for Bus 9, which was carrying the high schoolers who would transfer to Bus 4. I had a few minutes to wait. I parked the bus and took the ballots out of my pocket. I opened the top one. "Phil," it said.

I opened the next. "Phil."

The third: "Phil." The fourth: "Phil." The next and the next and the next: all the same. "Phil." "Phil." "Phil."

Phil won in a landslide. He received 97.4% of the votes. There might have been a few that did not say Phil, but those were pretty illegible, and looked like they might have been done by kindy-gartners who hadn't accepted any help in penmanship from the older kids.

There were only a dozen or so high schoolers on the second run that day. "I have ballots here for you," I said, "but I don't know if it's worth giving them out. The others have already voted, and you can't out-vote them. There's not enough of you."

"That's alright," came a voice from the back. "We know how they voted." "We all agree," said another voice.

I stopped at Pat Halsey's house that evening. I told her about the contest. Then I handed her the ballots. She began to read them. Then she began to cry. She cried and cried.

As for me, I was awestruck. Somewhere along the line, I had

forgotten that a bunch of people could do something absolutely right, and do it not out of self-interest of one type or another, but just because it was absolutely the right thing to do. And to find this whole bunch jammed into one old bus on one old country road...I almost could not believe it.

"But there it was," as Mark Twain used to say. It was hope... no, it was more than hope. It was a confirmation that the future of this wacko old race might have something optimistic or positive or even brilliant waiting in it. What a bunch of kids! I felt lucky. If these were the kind of kids I was going to be dealing with, I felt like I had found the pot of gold at the end of the rainbow.

If this was the kind of inclination that was in them, and if this inclination toward the good could be developed, we were going to be okay. They would still have to get through all the baggage of out-of-control hormones and pheromones and alcohol and drugs and everything else lurking around every corner for the next few years, but if the good in these hearts could be nurtured and protected, we were going to be okay.

October, 2008

Horace Squires drives Bus 7.
One day, I said to him,
"How's business, Horace?"
Without missing a beat, he replied,
"At first it was picking up;
then it began dropping off."

Well, I drove through September, and a beautiful month it was as far as the weather goes. I would arrive at the bus at 6:30 every morning; check it out, inside and out; make sure all the systems were in correct working order; warm it up; fill out my Bus Condition report; and be ready to roll. At exactly 7:00 AM, I would turn north on Pleasant Valley Road and pick up kids for five miles or so; turn left onto Irish Settlement Road and stay on that for about seven miles while it looped up into the hills and down again; and arrive with a busload of kids at Underhill Central School, where several hundred elementary school kids would debark. I could never understand that. I would pick these kids up singly or in pairs, just a few of them altogether, and somehow they would multiply on the bus. It was a constant source of amazement to me.

After the elementary school, I'd get back on Pleasant Valley Road again, heading south this time, bringing the middle schoolers and high schoolers down to Brown's River Middle School. The route took us through the bustling metropolis of Underhill Center, complete with Town Hall, St. Thomas Church, Underhill Country Store, the Underhill Center Post Office, Wells' Market, and a dozen or so houses. I would stop at the stop sign by the Underhill Country Store, look around carefully, and proceed down River Road toward the school some three miles distant. On the way I would wave to Phyllis in Bus 18 and Jack in Bus 22, heading past me toward the Central School.

Before I knew it I would be at Brown's River to drop the kids, and be back at Underhill Center by 8 AM. I'd check the bus for forgotten objects. You would not believe what kids could forget! Then I would sweep out the bus. (Yes, every run. Consider how your house would look if fifty people came into it every morning from a gravel road, dragging sand in. If I had saved all the sand I swept, by the end of the year I could have sold a ton of it to the road crew for use in winter.) After I swept the bus, I could go home. Not bad for a morning's work.

In the afternoon, at 2 PM sharp, I would drive over to Jericho Elementary School and join a line-up of seven buses. I'd pick up the Jericho kids and bring them home to Old Pump Road and Griswold Street and Snowflake Drive. Then I'd express back along Route 15 to Brown's River Middle School with the pre-schoolers, pick up the middle schoolers, head back into Underhill to pick up the elementary kids at Central at 3 PM, and the whole herd of us would hightail it up Pleasant Valley Road and down Irish Settlement Road once more, losing passengers all along the way.

Arriving empty at the end of the loop back at Central School (well, every day but one), I'd wait for Ron Buxton on Bus 9 to arrive with his load of high schoolers who would transfer to Phil. Then I'd loop-the-loop once more, bring the bus back to its parking space, sweep it out, look for coats, hats, pencils, lunch boxes, uneaten lunches, mp3 players, cell phones, whatever. I would inspect the bus, make sure the windows were closed, check it's systems, and be done for the day at about 4:30, generally.

And as September rolled by, I was feeling pretty good about my career change. On September 7th, there were rumblings about Freddie Mac and Fannie Mae. On the 9th, the Dow fell 300 points and 100 hedge funds were frozen. On the 15th, Lehman Brothers filed for bankruptcy. On the 16th, AIG was granted 85 billion in credit from the Federal Reserve. The US financial structure was being ripped apart and distributed worldwide by Barclay's and Nomura Holdings, among others. The Real Estate industry had ground to a halt. On the 24th, Senator John McCain suspended his presidential campaign to return to Washington in order to put an end to the crisis. Summarizing his announcement, he said, in part: "I am confident that before Monday morning..." Well, he was optimistic.

And I still had a job. Not too bad.

As I said, weather-wise, September was a grand old month, and everyone was looking forward to that most beautiful month in northern New England—October. October of the blue skies and white puff clouds, of the yellow and red and orange leaves painting entire hillsides with unimaginable beauty, of the sharp sting of the brisk northern winds of autumn, of the glistening morning frost shining in the sun...

On October 1st, it rained all day. On October 2nd, sleet. The whole cantankerous month was like that.

And the bus kept rolling.

Brody got on one day and said: "Are you happy it's Wednesday?"

"I'm happy it's *any* day," I replied. And I really was.

A chant rose from the first graders: "Chop at the bottom; chop at the top! Throw the rest, into the pot!" That went on long enough for me to try to figure it out and then give up, although I suppose it had to do with some kind of food preparation lesson.

Jim Bedell was building a new driveway off Irish Settlement. I stopped to wave. Jim jumped off his bulldozer, came over to the bus, grinning, and said "Are you likin' it, Dan?"

"I am likin' it, Jim!"

One Friday was Party Day. There were three parties going on in various home locations. Kids had invited hordes of friends from other bus routes. On they came with their bus passes. Ten extra to Mountain Road. Seven to Butler Road. A bunch more farther down on Irish Settlement. They were sitting three to a seat and having a grand old time squirming around and popping up and down and squealing. It was mayhem.

"Listen up!" I shouted. Nobody could hear me. "Listen up! Hey! Listen!" I shouted again. It took a while, and I have a loud voice when I want it. Finally it quieted. "Listen. I know it's crowded," I said. "Just do the best you can. Stop yelling. And stop popping up and down in the seats. It looks like Whack-a-Mole back there!"

Uh-Oh. Mistake. They loved the idea. "Whack-a-Mole! Whack-a-Mole!" they began to chant, popping up and down faster and higher. "I'll write you all up!" "Whack-a-Mole! Whack-a-Mole!" "Whack-a-Mole!" It was a grand party. I mean the one on the bus, not the ones they were going to. They still haven't forgotten it.

One afternoon, the Jericho first graders, kindy-gartners, and pre-schoolers were waiting for the other students to board for the afternoon run. The little kids grew bored waiting, so they decided to play that they were going to market to sell something. Soft whispers. "Okay, we're here. What can we sell now?" "Stardust. Let's sell stardust." And they did. And nobody knew what it was. And nobody checked to see if it was real. It was just like Wall Street!

Another day, a message came over the radio from a bus way out in the countryside: "Base, my bus may be on fire. There's smoke coming out from over the back right wheels."

Bob: "Clear the air!" Then "Pull over immediately!"
Driver: "I have."

Bob: "Get the kids off. Get them safe. Is there a safe place for them?"

Driver: "Side of the road. It's safe."

Bob: "Make sure it's safe."

Earl, the chief mechanic, driving another bus: "I can be there in two minutes."

Bob: "Good. Earl, check it out. The fire department and the troopers are on the way."

Earl: "Ten-four."

Bob: "Earl. The kids can transfer to your bus. You stay there until the situation's resolved."

A silence that seemed much longer than it really was, then—

Earl: "I'm here. The fire department's here. Everything's under control."

Bob: "Where's the driver? Where are the kids?"

Earl: "I don't see any kids. Driver's right here."

Bob: "Put her on." Driver comes on. "Where are the kids?"

Driver: "I don't know."

Bob, exploding: "What do you mean you don't know!"

Driver, laughing: "I can't find them. I stopped next to a corn field. It has a maze. They all ran into the maze."

Bob: "(deleted)"

Driver: "Oh, Bob. Don't worry. I'll go get 'em."

And she did. And they were fine. And so was the bus.

Speaking of corn, I had come to realize that most of these kids were natural cornballs. One day, I had an extra run down to the Flynn Theatre in Burlington, transporting a class of high school juniors to a presentation of "The Argonauts." I had no idea what "The Argonauts" was or were. It might have been a presentation of a classic Greek play. It might have been a heavy metal rock band. All I knew was what I had to know: get them to the Flynn; get out of there and up to Leddy Park with all the dozens of other buses converging on the Flynn at the same time; and wait 'til my number was called to go back and pick them up.

I did all that, and on the way home, I looked back in the Student Mirror at the rows of students. They *looked* like Argonauts, sitting there in their double rows. Rowdy. Cocky. Laughing. Jibing. All they needed was oars.

A bunch of guys all the way in the back were facing each other, knees together in the aisle. They were snapping their heads up and down, making their long hair fly out over their faces. With hair flailing, they looked like wet Argonauts. Something from the play? They would rock forward fast and the motion would heave their hair frontwards. Then they'd jerk backwards, snapping their necks back. The hair would fly back. Over and over. I decided to mention it to their teacher, who was sitting in the front seat. She turned and looked and turned back to me. "With what *could* be happening back there," she sighed, "I'll take it."

Based on this incident, I asked Bob if he could get a guidance counselor to attend one of our meetings and talk about which student behaviors appear to be absolutely aberrant but are actually normal in various developmental stages. I even had a title ready for the seminar. I called it "What the (insert favorite expletive here) are they doing *now*?" We never had that little seminar, but I wish we had. My own mind is a mystery to me; I can't imagine what goes on in theirs, but someday I'd like to try to find out. It would help.

I found that there is never anything you could call an uneventful day. There are three turkey herds in various spots on Irish Settlement Road. They are feeding in the cropped fields now, bulking up for winter. The geese are heading south in their Vees, honking as they go. Sometimes you can hear them garbelling really loud before you see them come down out of

the low-lying clouds. The Monarch butterflies are headed south, too, down to Mexico, or as far as they can get before they turn the job over to the next generation. The maples and ashes and beeches are turning the hillsides into magic mountains. And one sparkling afternoon with all the color in the leaves that you could ever want to see, just as we are passing Corbett's Corner, a big mama bear rambles right across the road in front of us. *Told* you we lived in the country.

In the middle of the month, I decided to assign seats for the afternoon runs. Had to. It might have been that party day that pushed things over the edge, but I had to get them to stop squirming around so much. They didn't like it; didn't like it at all. There was a great deal of whining and crabbing. "Why do we have to do this?" "None of the other bus drivers make us do this!" "I don't want to sit there, with him, with her, with them..." On and on and on it went, but they did it.

I did it for two reasons. One, as I said, was to stop all the squirming around. Two, just as important, was to identify them; to get to know them. I wanted to get to know them as individuals.

I had already gotten to know some of them. That's why Liam was sitting in the front seat. I'd heard enough of "Dan, Liam did this." "Dan, Liam did that." "Dan, Liam is crawling around under the seats again!" I suppose I should have written him up. But I didn't. He was only in second grade, for Pete's sake, and although he could be a source of mayhem at any instant, he was also very bright and had a really positive outlook on life. Just because he was into everything and couldn't sit still for a minute wasn't a reason to write him up, I figured, at least not without trying to get him off to a better start.

"So Liam. Do you know why you're sitting in the front seat for the next two weeks?"

"Yeah."

"Why?"

"I hit Brian."

"Why did you do that?"

"Because Brian hit Tyler."

"Why did he do that?"

"Because Tyler hit Kevin."

"Why...never mind." There wasn't any reason to go any further down that trail. "But you were the one who jumped over the back of the seat to get to Brian."

"No, I didn't."

"I saw you."

"Yeah."

"You can't do that. If you keep doing that, I'll have to write you up."

"Yeah. I'm sorry."

"So you know why you're up here. If I write you up, you'll stay up here forever."

"Yeah." (A big sigh). "I won't do it again."

Not for two weeks, anyway, I thought to myself. "We've got to work on this, Liam," I said.

"Yeah." Liam had a question.

"Can I hit Tyler?"

"Of course not. Why would you want to hit Tyler?"

"He's my brother."

One day, when I'd brought the bus in for fuel and an adjustment to the windshield wiper, Craig asked me if I was having any trouble with any of the kids. I told him about Liam, his seat-jumping and crawling, and my assigning him to the front seat. Craig thought I had handled it fairly well. "The important thing," Craig said, "is that you let him know what he's up there for. Some drivers just stick them up there and don't tell them. Doesn't do any good. Got to tell them." I told him how I was telling Liam that we had to work on this. Craig thought this was good. So did Earl.

I began to realize that I didn't know anything about these kids as students. I didn't know anything about what went on inside those buildings I delivered them to every day. I didn't know if they were considered bright or slow or average; what their individual talents were; what talents were being hidden; what talents developed. I didn't know anything about what was happening 'inside the box.' All I knew was that they were terrific individuals, and that each of them got up every day and slogged forward through it all, sometimes in a deep funk, but always filled with hope, I guess, and wonderment at it all. Just like the rest of us.

Except on a 'sugar day.' Sometimes whole classes would be treated to candy at the end of a day, and boy, could you tell the difference. Sometimes individuals would get their hands on some just before they left school, somehow. Whatever—whether individual or group—they would go sky-high. If you called them on some behavior, they'd just say "Sugar!" and laugh their heads off.

There's a story that somewhere up in the Northeast Kingdom of Vermont, there once was a school that had a policy of filling the kids with candy at the end of every Friday. The kids would get on the buses on a vast sugar high. Mayhem would follow. The bus drivers spoke to the teachers about it, but no matter how many times they brought up the problem, the candy distribution continued. This made Friday afternoons really interesting for the drivers, to the point where they decided to do something about it. They decided to retaliate. So one Halloween morning, as the kids got off the buses, each was handed a big sack of candy to take in to school with them.

That afternoon, the kids got back on the buses. They were really quiet, docile, dopey, down off their sugar highs. They looked exhausted. So did their teachers. The point was made. The Friday afternoon candy distribution stopped, never to be seen or heard from again.

Perhaps it was in honor of those brave bus drivers in the Kingdom that on Hallowe'en, Horace, the driver of Bus 7, was wearing a t-shirt that bore the legend: **"It's Halloween. The Zombies are out looking for some brains. Don't worry. You're safe."**

HAPPY HALLOWE'EN !!

November, 2008

Phil the Bus was in the shop for November inspection and maintenance, I stopped by to see how everything was going. Craig was working on it, and I asked him if he had found anything wrong.
"No," says Craig,
"Just a nut loose behind the wheel."

So much happened in November that it should have had an extra day in it. For one thing, October, which should have been bright and snappy, had been pretty miserable. November, which is traditionally the bleakest month of the year, dawned bright and beautiful, and stayed that way for a good part of itself. That was for starters.

On Saturday, November 1st, we all turned back the clocks, and the days changed considerably. It was almost as if the earth had suddenly gotten serious about things. And serious things were afoot. For one thing, on Monday, Madison, a ninth grader, showed up for the afternoon run with a baby. It was a plastic baby, programmed to wake screaming in the middle of the night, several times, wanting and needing and leaking like all get-out. Each ninth grader got to carry the baby around for a couple of days and nights at a stretch. It was supposed to teach them the seriousness of having and caring for a baby. I believe it did. Madison, who was the first ninth grader on our bus to get the baby, got on the bus pretty bleary-eyed on Tuesday and Wednesday. When I asked her how it was going, she just rolled her eyes.

The next big event, of course, was Election Day. John McCain had never recovered from his ill-advised March on Washington. The nation elected Barack Obama—a community organizer, attorney, law professor, and U.S. Senator from Illinois—and the nation and the world waited to see what would happen next.

What happened was a spate of illnesses on the bus. "Where's your brother?" "Got a rash." Where's Scott?" "Has a temperature. 107." "Oh?" "Where's Sean?" "He's got pink-eye." Someone else was out with something terrible, but what it was I don't recall at present. Probably for the best, for your sake.

On Friday the 7th, Liam announced excitedly, "There are slugs all over our driveway!"

The next weekend was "Youth Hunting Weekend." On Monday, Chuck Conklin, a sixth grader, proudly showed off a picture of his eight-point buck. To everyone. Everyone except Liam was mightily impressed. Liam was sullen and already planning for next year. All he had gotten was a bob-white, and he was having a fit that he hadn't nailed a deer. Later his grandfather said to me, "What a kid! Six years old, first time out, he gets a bird! The kid's good." Liam was at home in the woods. For some reason, he had the ability to be as silent and stealthy as a cat in the woods. Good for him, but it didn't satisfy him. Nope.

Also on Monday, on the afternoon run, I heard the first wispy strains of "Jingle Bells." Christmas came the next day for AIG. To celebrate Veterans' Day, I guess, the government gave the corporation a total of $150 billion dollars. Starbucks' net was down 97%. The AMEX was in the bucket. It was the night of The Hunter's Moon, and all the financial gremlins were out in force, trying to trip up as many companies and individuals as possible. So much for de-regulation.

On Wednesday the 12th, there was snow on the top of Mt. Mansfield, the first of the season. Also on that day, Nicole asked when the other bus drivers were going to assign seats. It was a warning signal, the first blip on the radar of things to come.

On Thursday the 13th, the armada showed up in force: Paige, Nicole, and Morgan, backed up by Pete. They brought a list of what they liked and didn't like about the bus. They also brought a list of what they wanted changed. It was in the form of a petition signed by the four of them and a few others they had rounded up. The petition stated that they wanted the right to change seats whenever the bus was stopped; the right to eat and drink "as long as we don't make a mess"; and no assigned seats. Actually, the petition said "no assin seats," which I thought really summed up the core of their requests. No assin seats, ever.

When I went to Bob Magee to ask his advice on allowing leniency on the bus rules, Bob said, laughing, "Leave it to Underhill to come up with a petition!" Then he reflected and said, "Tell them no on changing seats and food and drink," he said. "That's simply against the rules. But on the assigned seats...that's up to you. It's your bus. You do what you think is necessary. You make the rules. Play it as it comes."

I wanted to keep them sitting where they were. I still hadn't learned all of their names, and I wanted to do that, so I wanted to keep them in place for a while longer.

On Friday the 14th, nobody asked me anything. It was Report Card Day, and almost everybody was really quiet.

The next Monday, the 17th, I was again approached by the Committee of Four on the homebound trip while we were waiting for the elementary kids to board at Central School. I gave them the bad news. "About changing seats and drinking and eating," I said, "forget it. It's against the rules. See? The rules are right up there." I pointed to Bob's Rules pasted to the front of the bus. They all sat in the front of the bus (an infraction, in itself, of my "assigned seat" rule, but I didn't care; I was enjoying this), and they read the rules.

"What does c-o-u-r-t-e-o-u-s mean?" Morgan asked. Paige said, "I don't understand how you get up at six o'clock every morning to drive this bus." "I don't get up at six," I said. "I get up at five." "What do you do during the day," asked Nicole. "Just wait around?" Well, not quite, young lady, I thought, laughing to myself. I pointed to the rules sign. "Rule number ten," I said. "Do not distract the driver." By this time, the elementary kids had come on board and were milling around in the aisle like a school of guppies, wondering why these big middle schoolers were sitting in their seats.

"As for the assigned seats," I said, "I'll have to think about that for a bit. Maybe we can work something out. But not now. Right now you're in seats assigned to these elementary kids. Get back to your assigned seats, and we can work on this over the next few days."

They left, and onward we drove.

Tuesday, November 18th—Winter signed in today with a warning of things to come. The snow started as I drove down the hill to the bus. By the time I had it started, inspected, and warmed up, there might have been a half-inch on the ground. It continued to snow as I traveled north on Pleasant Valley Road, until it had accumulated perhaps an inch. Then it stopped.

But this snow showed no signs of melting. It clung to the asphalt, and I had to proceed with extreme caution. As I drove up Pleasant Valley, the radio chatter began between the buses and Base, and bus to bus, warning of conditions. There were some buses in trouble. One was stopped already on Packard Road in Jericho, up near the top, near Orr Road, and it wasn't about to move until the town trucks came by and sanded. The

driver could see down the hill to where a car had sailed off the road and into the trees. Farther down, a car spun sideways. Those kids would to be late today, no question about that.

I turned onto Irish Settlement. Conditions here weren't too bad. The dirt road gave more grip than the asphalt, and I breathed a bit easier. The kids got on and took their seats just like it was a normal day. The road felt good. But all the while, a constant stream of reports came over the intercom: I-89 was closed. Cars were off the road all along Brown's Trace. Richmond was a total disaster, with buses going every which way trying to find open routes to Camel's Hump Middle School. Alternate routes had to be taken and some parents had to be informed their kids would have no bus today.

There was an excellent, comprehensive contingency plan in place for snow days, but this little squall came after everything—

the buses, the drivers, the teachers, the students, the administrators, life in general—was already in motion. The town road crews had no time to get into position. The squall had not been predicted, and the town trucks were still in their yards, filling up with sand and salt. They were quick about it, but the storm was quicker.

I seemed to be doing fine, but as I approached Flynn Hill on Irish Settlement just south of Donovan Road, I could feel the quality of the snow cover change. I remembered what Alan had told me—this hill, although it didn't look like much, was a bear in snow. He'd advised that at any time there was snow, I back up a few hundred feet to where the road leveled out and get a running start so that by the time I hit the bottom of the hill, I'd have enough momentum to get to the top.

I picked up the Donovan kids at their road and looked back to see if there was any traffic. There was. There were three cars in back of me. I decided to go forward. After all, it was only an inch of snow. What could happen?

Going up the hill, I was suddenly in the midst of a perfect storm of poor conditions. First, I was driving a "loaner" bus. Phil—Bus #4—was in for maintenance, so I didn't have the feel of this bus like I might have had with Phil. Second, I couldn't back up because of the traffic behind me. (I know better now; I would have had that traffic back up and let me get a better start). So, third, I had to start climbing the hill cold from a standing position. Fourth, I had never driven a bus in snow before.

I started out fine. The bus chugged along up the hill like it was a nice spring day in the middle of May. Then the back end slid out. Suddenly, the bus was almost sideways, then it began to slip down the hill. I managed to maneuver it off to the side, to the shallow ditch. I aimed the front wheels where I thought I should go and hit the accelerator. Good. The bus started forward, and I got it maybe another thirty feet up the hill. Then it slipped sideways again and started down. I got it into the ditch again where there was more loose gravel. This time, when I started up, I kept the left wheels in the ditch. That gave me traction. Slipping and throwing up gravel all the way, I finally made it to the top, and that was that. I started breathing again, and so did the kids, who had been absolutely silent the whole time. I realized that all the way up the hill, you could have heard a pin drop in that bus. I may have started breathing at the top of that hill, myself, but my heart was still pounding and the adrenalin was coursing around my body like crazy.

I finished the route, picking up an additional five or so kids along the way, pulled up at the Underhill Central School, and cut the engine. As the elementary kids disembarked, Carolyn Kelley crossed in front of the bus with Liam and Tyler in tow. I realized that she had been driving one of the cars behind the bus. As she crossed, she grinned, gave me the thumbs-up sign, and said "Nice driving!" I managed to grin back at her, and a bit of a big weight slipped off my shoulders. I relaxed and drove on to Brown's River, where the rest of the students got off.

I felt even better the next day when, at the end of a scheduled drivers' meeting, Bob Magee tapped me on the shoulder and said, "You know how parents call to complain about the bus driver. Well, it's always a pleasure to tell a driver about a call that says you did something right. Carolyn Kelley called and said she was in back of you yesterday when you took that hill, and she thought you did a great job."

I was mighty pleased.

The next two days were parent conference days, which meant half-days of school. We drove the kids to school and then turned around and a couple of hours later, we brought them home again, all except the ones that were being hung up by their thumbs by their parents or teachers. So these were early days, mini-vacation hours, and very much appreciated by me and, I suspect, by all the other drivers as well.

And then it was Thanksgiving vacation.

It was not the best of Thanksgivings at my house. A week before, Emily had called and told us that her mother, Shelley, was not doing well. She was in St. Barnabas Hospital down in New Jersey. Emily said that her systems seemed to be shutting down.

Shelley had been afflicted with a combination of debilitating symptoms for at least ten years. She was finally diagnosed with Sjogren's disease. Sjogren's is an extraordinarily vicious autoimmune disorder—a disease that causes the immune system to attack its own body. Its cause is unknown. There is no cure. It can link with other diseases, especially rheumatic diseases, and its symptoms can overlap with others. Usually, a number of specialists have to be consulted before a final diagnosis is obtained. It can affect the nervous system, blood vessels, and many of the major organs in the body.

We had watched Shelley progress from walking with a cane to a walker, then to a wheelchair, then to the use of oxygen. Now she was once again in the hospital. She wanted to see us, and we wanted to see her.

Joanie and Shelley had met in Manhattan back in the late sixties. Joanie had gone there to take a Master's Degree in Social Work at Fordham University. Shelley had arrived to work in publishing. They'd become fast friends. Joanie was Shelley's maid of honor at her wedding. The friendship had lasted and deepened over the years. Shelley abandoned the publishing world for a career in law. While she was in law school, she was one of three members of the Moot Court Competition team the year that Fordham won the national championship.

After law school, she worked for a time as an Assistant

District Attorney in the Southern District of New York, serving under the legendary Robert Morganthau. And she was such a friend to so many people. She had possibly the best memory in the world. She always remembered your birthday, anniversary, special events in your life; and she did this for seemingly dozens of relatives and friends. It was uncanny. She never missed. All that information was in her head. She could come out with it any time you asked. Our house was full of wonderful, thoughtful gifts she had bestowed on us over the years.

There was no way we were not going down to New Jersey to see Shelley. We spent Thanksgiving packing, left the Friday after Thanksgiving, found a reasonably decent motel off an interstate, and went to the hospital. Joanie brought her small bedside Celtic harp with her. When we went into Shelley's room, Shelley tried to jump for joy, but all she could do was wiggle her legs a little and make a kind of muffled sound that sounded like "You came!" That's all she could do. But her eyes sparkled, and she could smile, even with all the tubes connected to her.

Joanie played for close to two hours. She had taken a course in Harp Therapy, where she learned how to play for people in hospital settings. She had played for years at Fletcher Allen Hospital in Burlington in many different situations—oncology, dialysis, psychiatric, palliative care—and now she poured out everything she knew for Shelley.

And then we said goodbye and left, and Shelley slept.

Emily called us a few days later. Shelley had died. She was sixty years old. The funeral was to be in two days in Philadelphia, the burial in her family plot. There was no way we would be able to attend, but many people were in the same situation, and so a memorial service would be held in New Jersey in February. We would go there.

December, 2008

...and the bus rolled on.

It rolled on through the light and darkness of December. It rolled on beneath blue skies and low purple clouds. It rolled on through the ever-deepening darkness heading toward the solstice, rolling with the earth through the dark of space toward the far-off promise of longer, lighter days, the promise of better times to come. And always, accompanying the darkness of the year was the darkness of the loss of our great good friend Shelley.

But there was also light. There was light enough to see the changing colors of the farmland along River Road; light enough to see the disappearing corn stubble, covered little by little by the December snows, snows that seemed to come slowly, as little as an inch a day. There was enough light to see the deepening grayness of the wooded hillsides; the trees freezing themselves tight against the oncoming winter.

Monday, December 1st, held a dark and stormy pre-dawn start for the bus. I got down to it early to make sure everything was fit, that I had enough time to warm it up. It took a while.

The thermometer said 8° when I left the house. It was still dark when I pulled onto the road at 7 o'clock, the bus groaning from several different places as it righted itself. But as I drove on and on into the dark, there was brightness there. People had taken the opportunity of the weekend to put up their Christmas lights. There they were as you came around bends and over hills, lights shining in the morning darkness. See! Earth, we are ready. We are adding light to you. Now you get going. There's a new birth coming. The world will be bright again. We are doing our part. Come on. Get cracking. Lighten up!

And life was going on in its constantly mysterious ways. On December 8th, for instance, a day which had been at -2° when I arrived at the bus, I saw two wings of geese, as big as any wings I had ever seen, flying high up at 9 AM and again at noon. What were they doing here now? They should have been gone a long time ago. Well, maybe not. Maybe they knew something I didn't know. I hoped they did. I hoped they weren't mistaken; hadn't let themselves be trapped in the steel-cold fist of Old Man Winter.

I was delighted that I was here to witness this oncoming winter. As Tennyson said, "It little profits that an idle king..." just sit around and stew in his own juice while he waited for... for...whatever final mystery was coming down the pike to get him. No, the thing to do was to get up early and get out and get on with it, go out and do something, drive a bus to get the day started off right, for instance.

And also, there were the constant little mysteries to ponder, instead of the Great Eternal ones. Like the mysterious behavior of kids. Like the mysterious behavior of Dennis, who one afternoon sat there and beat himself over the head over and over and over again with a spiral-bound notebook. Hard. I couldn't figure out what he was doing, so I finally asked. "Why are you doing that, Dennis?" With no embarrassment, with no shoulder shrugging or any other signs of discomfort, he looked me in the eye and said, "I felt like it." He didn't say anything about not knowing why he was doing it, he was just doing it. It was just another part of life to move through and see what it would do. Well, why not?

And so the bus coursed through the early December days until Friday, the 12th. I was getting ready to leave the house to drive when the call came at 5:35 AM. "Dan?" "Yuh."

"It's Alan." "Mornin'." "G'morning." A slight pause, then, "No school today." I looked out the window. It was snowing. It was snowing a lot. It was a Snow Day! I had heard all about these mythical Snow Days, and here was one. So they weren't just myths after all! Yee-hah! And what a day for it. A Friday. Suddenly a really good, useful, three-day weekend just when I needed it.

I had a lot to do. I began immediately to turn Friday into Saturday. I got 21 papers off my desk, did the laundry, got the wood in, the dog walked, the decks shoveled, and started baking my famous Christmas chocolate chip cookies. Evidently, the whole northern part of the state was pretty much shut down.

So Joanie was home. And she got a lot of stuff done, too. Probably more than I did. In the early afternoon, she wrapped up a copy of The Greatest Generation, made an appointment with Laurie (who had had a lot of cancellations), went out to get her hair cut, and stopped at the post office (the mail must go through) to mail the book to Ben (ninety-two and still going strong) over in England.

While I was baking my cookies, I listened to the radio—an interview with Clint Eastwood. "A horse is a twelve-hundred pound animal with a brain the size of a hickory nut," he said to Terri Gross on PBS. "Very early you learn that he is not going to contribute a lot to the ride." Well, I thought, multiply that by thirty and you have a 36,000 pound school bus that has a computer but that nevertheless fishtails like a 1953 Plymouth. I would say that you can expect as much from the bus as Eastwood expected from a horse.

I enjoyed making these comparisons. I had already compared the bus to a train, an airplane, and a giant, megasized New York yellow cab. It started with the train. I noticed the first time I got into the bus that everybody waves to you. Remember the semi driver who nodded to me the first day I was driving? Well, *everybody* waves to you. They will be driving with one hand on their cell phone and the other holding a cup of coffee and they'll see you coming and nod or wave with their free pinky. They will be walking, jogging, running, meandering, bicycling, taking their dogs out, pushing baby strollers, and they will wave.

"You better wave back," said Alan. "It's part of your job description." I believe it is. Perhaps not written, but it's there. People get really bummed out if you don't initiate a wave or at least wave back. I finally ended up waving at every car that came down the road so I wouldn't disappoint anyone, because—and I don't know how I missed this during the past twenty-eight years I had been living here—I had never bothered to memorize the cars of everybody I knew. Consequently, I never knew who was coming toward me. But, I began to learn them, almost as fast as I was learning the names of all of the kids. I was amazed to realize just how many people I knew in town. This waving business was fun!

That was when it hit me. People wave to the school bus just like they used to wave to the engineers and conductors on the classic old steam locomotives that hauled those great old, long freight trains through town. Boy. I remembered doing that. But now very few people, comparatively, live near the tracks. So they have transferred their daily greetings from the engineers to the school bus drivers. There are valid comparisons here:

> First, we both haul some very valuable freight.
>
> Second, we show up pretty close to on-the-minute every day. I'm not saying we're to-the-second, but pretty close. Close enough that people can see us coming, check their watches, and go, "Yup. There's the three-forty-three."
>
> Third, we are standard members of the community. We are time-tested ties to the towns, kind of like the road crew and the town clerk and the select board and the post office mail carriers and the guys up on the telephone poles. We are part of the apparatus that keeps the community going. In this day and age, you can't run a community without school buses.
>
> Fourth, did you ever notice how much these school buses look like locomotive engines?

So, okay. Sometimes I feel like a locomotive engineer. Allow me my fantasy. Sometimes after I get all the kids home on the afternoon run, I sing "The Wabash Cannonball" to myself. At the top of my lungs:

> Listen to the jingle, the rumble,
>   and the roar.
> She rolls along the woodlands,
>   through the hills and by the shore.
> Hear the mighty rush of engines,
>   hear the hobo's lonely squall
> Echo through the jungles,
>   'It's the Wabash Cannonball!'

Alright, I'll tell you everything. I also sing "Muleskinner Blues" a lot. And "The Ox-Driving Song," too. Odetta's version. "The Ox-Driving Song" is really good in mud season, when you're wrestling the wheel and weaving through foot-deep, mud-filled potholes that have suddenly sprung up like the earth is about to start grinding and cracking apart while creating a cold, mud soup. "When we got West, the hills were steep; t'would make a gentle person weep; to hear me cuss, and pop my whip; and make those oxen pull and slip..."

So much for the train comparison. I think it's really valid. Now how about the New York City yellow cab? Well, both vehicles are yellow. How's that for starters? And nobody in his right mind will go near either of them. You cannot win an argument with either a school bus or a yellow cab. True, a bus can't do everything a yellow cab can do. It cannot make it across midtown Manhattan in three minutes during rush hour traffic while customers cringe in horror and pedestrians dive for cover. But it can just sit there while you grind pieces off your car trying to drive through its rear bumper. Thus, they are both extraordinarily formidable vehicles.

Okay, how about the planes? (Whoa! Where is this guy going? Some kind of a macho fantasy ride?) Well, why not? I'm standing here waiting for the cookies to bake, remember? How's that for macho? Anyway, the planes. If you've ever watched seven buses pile into the circular drive in front of Jericho Elementary School and load up and take off—oh, look at that, he said 'take off'; should we allow this lunatic to drive our children around?—yes, vroom on their engines and start to move out, it's easy to see them as World War II bombers headed for Germany, a la the old war movie "Twelve O'Clock High." Well, just look at them. They look like old 1940s C-47s without wings. They're actually in better shape than those old C-47s, too. I remember once, during the mid-sixties, in the middle of a flight from St. Croix to St. Thomas down in the Virgin Islands, I looked out the window and noticed a number of rivets in the wing dancing up and down with the vibrations. After we touched down, on the way out, I told the stewardess about them. She leaned way back against the fuselage of the plane and started slumping to the floor. I guess she didn't know about the rivets.

I thought it was pretty much usual for a C-47 to do that. I'm pretty sure Earl would never let rivets pop like that on one of his buses.

Anyway, here goes the squadron of wingless yellow C-47s down Route 15, just about to sprout wings and take to the air... pocketa-pocketa-pocketa...

So Eastwood is finished talking about the horses, and the cookies are baked, and the news is on: Republican Senators down in Washington are celebrating our Snow Day too, by trying to destroy the United Auto Workers. Ho Ho Ho, Merry Christmas!

And actually, it was a great start to the Holiday Season. That Sunday was my 68th birthday. 68. And that was just the start of the festivities. The kids on my bus and their parents didn't know it had just been my birthday. They had begun celebrating the other big birthday of the month—the one coming up on the 25th. And boy, did they celebrate it. I had presents coming in the door every day, mostly having to do with sugar in as many forms as possible. It was an exuberance of sugar! An extravaganza of sugar! I got gooey breakfast buns with walnut topping. White fudge so rich it tasted like pure butter. Champlain Chocolates. Snowflake Chocolates. Truffles. Homemade cookies. Cookies, cookies, cookies, cookies, cookies, cookies. Crackle. A box of Russell Stover candy. Maple syrup sugared off on Irish Settlement Road. CranApple relish. Two sugar Santas and four homemade truffles. A bag of chocolate biscotti. Danish cookies. Candy. Candy. Shortbread. Caramelized mixed nuts—a really nice mixture, too. And a big hug from Jenny (five years old).

How wonderful it was! What a wonderful outpouring of happiness was mine. Wonderful, grand gifts from great, grand hearts. How lucky I felt simply to have been a part of this Christmas with you. Thank you, my friends!

Merry Christmas, everyone! And the sleigh...I mean the bus...disappeared into the night of the 24th, not to re-appear until January of 2009.

January, 2009

...and have I told you just how cold it can get on a cloudless pitch-black night in the middle of winter just before morning when the sun is a distant memory on the horizon of the night before, without a hint of another morning ever to come again? When it's six o'clock in the morning and the temperature is maybe 22 below and there's a foot of snow on the ground and the snow is frozen into ridges in the parking lot, and even though the bus has been plugged in all night to keep the engine from freezing up entirely, when you open the door and step up into that frozen yellow cavernous space, it's as dark and cold and stiff and still as a freezer with the door shut and the lights off. And you turn the key in the ignition and the engine moans and groans and finally turns over, and falters, and your heart jumps because what if it doesn't turn over, and finally it catches and it doesn't roar into life but just sort of chugs along half-dead for the first couple of minutes, and it's a long time before you dare to turn on any of the switches because the slightest strain on the battery might send it over the edge into oblivion and then what would you do when the thing is as dead as a doornail and you're standing there looking down at the driver's seat but you don't dare sit down because you'll freeze to the thing and even with your really good warm thick gloves if you touch the steering wheel the cold will come through the gloves and numb your hands? Have I told you that? Well, let me tell you: it can get pretty damn cold.

Things pile up in the winter. What can happen, happens. Moisture clogs the air brake systems. Thermostats fail. Roof fixtures leak. Exhaust systems rust out. Back emergency doors freeze up. Computers go whacky. Gauges stop working. Dashboard components freeze. Wires come loose. Windshield wipers break under ice build-up. Buses just plain stop running in the cold. The oddest things can happen. One morning, the 16th, it was 22 below at 5:30 AM when I got down to old Phil the Bus. I got there early because I wanted to be sure I'd have it warmed up with enough time to drive over to the garage at MMU and fuel up. It didn't really need it. I had about 2/3rd of a tank, but I wanted to keep it topped off. A full tank helps to keep the diesel fuel from turning into a sludge-like mass. Besides, it was so cold I thought I might be picking up some really frozen kids, and I wanted the bus to be warm for them. They're a tough bunch of Vermont mountain kids, but there are limits.

So I warmed it up for a good spell and then went through the checklist. Last on the list was the warning system—the reds—which begin to flash when you open the doors. Well, they didn't flash this morning, but not because they weren't working. They didn't flash because the doors didn't open. The doors didn't open because the air system that activates them hadn't built up enough pressure to function.. The cold was so intense it had shrunk the compressed air molecules. I guessed that was it. But now I had another reason to go over to the shop. I needed to find a mechanic.

I started over, gingerly. You can break things at 22 below if you aren't careful. Metal gets stressed. So I moved slowly down River Road, maybe 30 to 35 mph, then on to Route 15, and turned left onto Brown's Trace. Oh, it was bitter out. It was the kind of brittle night that shatters things; the kind of night that makes you think you're walking on the dark side of the moon.

When I got to the garage, I pulled up and opened the doors. Yes, they opened fine. The air molecules that had shrunk were warmed up in the twenty minutes it took to arrive at the high school. The bus and its air systems were heated enough to work properly now. This sort of thing can happen in the bitter cold, even with buses that have two systems of back-up heaters. I fueled up and headed back to Underhill with Phil good and warm and running in top-notch condition. By the time I got back, there was a trace of light in the East and a new day was on its way, cold as it might be.

But I'm getting ahead of myself. Let's return to the real business of driving a bus—politics.

You may recall that before Christmas broke in with all its mesmerizing ability to move people's minds to different places, I was engaged in talks regarding assigned seating, the right to change seats, eat, drink, be merry, and install a system of true anarchy in the bus. I had told the Committee on Assin Seats that I would mull over their request and get back to them. Well, I had done that, in part. I had conveyed the message about eating and drinking. I had set aside the question of assigned seats.

I knew the question was still open. There was a lot of talk going on in the back of the bus all through December. At times, it was really intense. At times, it looked like preparations for the Oldest Established Permanent Floating Crap Game in New York were being made. I knew they were plotting something back there, but I didn't know what.

But here it was January 2nd, the first day of class in the New Year, and up from the back of the bus came a new petition, carrying a message of

CLASS WARFARE

Yes. Class warfare. It was a petition signed by all the seventh and eighth graders. They wanted territory. Homeward bound on the afternoon bus, they wanted control of the four back seats. They wanted them reserved for themselves, "and for anybody we want to invite back there." I looked at their petition. It was well-written—better-written, at any rate, than the fifth-grade petition. Signed by all of them. Solidarity forever. In

Union there is Strength. E Pluribus Unum. It made me think.

It made me think back to my own time in school. I remembered how important classes were. That is where you made the vast majority of your friends. They were important friends, your classmates. They knew what you were going through. Before you met other students through clubs or activities or sports, you had your classmates. And when things got tough, that's where you went—back to your classmates.

So I looked at their petition seriously. By granting this petition, I would acknowledge their importance. This arrangement would grant them status. It would grant them semi-autonomy. To me, it meant stability in the back of the bus. And what would I get out of it beyond stability? For one thing, it would do a lot toward short-circuiting the Anarchy Petition brought by the fifth graders.

The seventh and eighth graders brought me the petition on the morning run. I granted their petition in the afternoon. When they got on the bus, I announced: "From now until the end of the school year, if all goes well and if you are all well-behaved, the seventh and eighth graders have the following seats: 19, 20, 21, 22, 23, 24, and half of Seat 17."

"No assigned seats?"

"Sit where you want, as long as there's no trouble. That's your territory. You've got to control it, or else I'll go back to the assigned seats. Got it?"

"Solid!"

There was a surge in the back of the bus as seats were claimed by means of a status scramble that only the participants would ever fully understand. A pecking order was quickly established, and it quickly pecked order out of chaos. That was one happy group of campers that rode home that night, those seventh and eighth graders.

That was Tuesday. On Friday came another petition, this one from...well, you know where it came from. From the fourth and fifth graders. “We want seats 9, 10, 11, 12, and half of 13,” said Paige, Nicole, Morgan, Pete, and Patrick, almost in chorus.

I should have known. This was a good thing. More territory was being established. What about the sixth grade? The sixth grade was fine. Cool. Plenty of room between the 7-8 and 4-5 groups. Their territory was automatically established by a sub-treaty between them and the fourth and fifth graders, I supposed. Whatever, when I asked them about it, they were fine with it.

And so it went down the line, the grades straightening themselves out, always top to bottom, always to the disadvantage of the younger, smaller kids. The strong pushed against the weak, and the weak moved against the weaker. At the same time, there were always attempts at upward mobility, which generally caused an uproar from those who were being impacted. But in practice, the class lines were porous. Upward mobility was invited in some cases, denied in others. Gad! It was just like a medieval feudal society. The Magna Carta had been granted, and the realm leapt forward into a new day of democracy and freedom. A new society was being formed right in front of my eyes, or behind my ears at least. It was fascinating. And I could study it every day while it lasted. It lasted a decent amount of time, too.

Overall, January was a month of surprises and changes, but nothing that happened on the bus could compare with what was happening outside of it. On January 15th, the media was suddenly filled with reports that tumbled all over each other in quick succession.

A US Air jet climbing out of LaGuardia Airport in New York had lost power in both engines. It was trying to glide to a landing at another airport. It couldn't make it. It was down in the Hudson. It was floating in the Hudson River. The emergency doors opened. People streamed out of the plane onto its wings. They stood there in the freezing water, lined up one next to another, waiting. Waiting for what? Waiting for the plane to go down? Waiting for death in the frigid water? No, they were waiting for the boats to come to get them. New York City Fire Department fireboats were on their way. Ferries from New York were coming. Circle Line tourist cruise boats were coming. And they did it. They did it quickly and well, and people took pictures of the whole thing. The whole world could watch as, one by one, the passengers walked or were helped off the wings of the plane and onto the ferries and boats. And just like it was supposed to be, the last one off that plane was the captain, Chesley B. "Sully" Sullenberger.

They called it "The Miracle on the Hudson," and I believed it was. The whole nation believed it was. There was something absolutely eerie about it. It was almost like it represented the United States itself. Here we were, a nation beset by a crisis that seemed to go on and on, deeper and deeper; and suddenly we looked up and found that we had a hero among us, a hero who could pilot a powerless plane into a river, get it to float, get all his passengers and crew off safely, and like courageous captains of old, make sure everybody was taken care of before he left his ship himself. If Hollywood had presented this scenario in a movie, nobody would have believed it. But there it was. We had a hero.

Was this an omen? Might there be another hero in the wings? Might there be a new President with the ability to turn our vast Ship of State onto a new course of hope and prosperity, and leave behind the morass of unbridled financial deregulation and depravity that had obviously not worked?

Soon, we thought, we would find out. On January 20th, President Barack Obama took the oath of office. That day happened to be a half-day for the senior high students, who were in the middle of exams. We were supposed to pick them up at 12:30 and get them home, a schedule that conflicted somewhat with the inauguration. But I turned on the radio as the half-dozen or so kids filed onto the bus, their exams still buzzing around their brains. We were able to hear just the very last of President Obama's speech, and a poem, and a benediction, and by the time the Navy's Sea Chanters started the Star-Spangled Banner, we were zipping down Pleasant Valley Road.

I sensed something amiss in the back of the bus, and I looked into the Student Mirror. Diedre was standing up. I hit the brakes gently, came almost to a stop, and yelled, "Are you alright? What's the matter?"

"The Anthem," she said. The others were beginning to stand also. I pulled the bus over at Corbett Corners Road, pulled on the flashers, and there we sat, stood, until the anthem was finished. Then they all sat down and we resumed our journey.

On the 26th, Pfizer announced 8,000 jobs would be cut; Sprint, another 8,000; Home Depot, 7,000; Caterpillar, 5,000 plus 2,500 buyouts. Prior to this, Caterpillar had let go 4,000 workers in addition to 8,000 additional contract workers. On this day, over 70,000 job cuts were announced. In 2008, 2.6 million jobs had been lost. President Obama was going to have his work cut out for him.

On the 27th, a blizzard approached. We went to school as usual. Then, were we given the word that there would be early dismissal at 11:30 AM. Back we drove through the gathering storm, which was expected to be at its height between 2 and 7 PM. Suddenly, all hell broke loose—not with the storm, but with the delivery of students. The well-tuned early dismissal routine couldn't cope with parents trapped in traffic jams down in Burlington and Essex Junction.

But all's well that ends well. We finally got them home, or to safe places that could get them home. Then we all hunkered down for a long winter's night, got up early, brushed off the snow, and started driving again.

The month ended the way it began, with class warfare. This time, it was the tiniest ones— the pre-schoolers—who sent up a howl. Brianna and Lucas, the two four-year-olds I bring from their Jericho Elementary Pre-School class to their Underhill homes, couldn't stand it any more. The ride was getting long for four-year-olds, and they were bored to tears. So to pass the time, they started up a sort of a howling yowl. I mean a LOUD yowling howl. Then they'd break to giggle, and start it up again, louder than ever. It was sort of a shriek this time, and they loved it, so they kept it going, rolling along in the highest decibels they could manage, despite all the warnings and admonitions I gave them.

We stopped at Brown's River and I loaded the middle school students and headed toward Underhill Central. The wolf-pack broke into a rollicking yowl again. Boy, were they having fun! But nobody else was. In the back of the bus, smiles of amusement turned to looks of pain. Brianna and Lucas, up in Seat 1 where I could supposedly keep an eye on them, loved the effect they were having. The decibels went up even higher. Higher. Higher. It was like Jimi Hendricks at Woodstock.

Before I even realized she was out of her seat (breaking every rule ever written about staying in your seat while the bus is moving), Nicole was up the aisle and sitting in Seat 2, across from the wolf-pack. She leaned across the aisle and whispered to them. Suddenly, they were completely quiet. Their heads were pressed against the seat-back in front of them. They were motionless. Nicole got up again and returned to her seat. The wolf-pack remained quiet and motionless for the duration of the ride.

Later, after I dropped the two of them off, I said to Nicole, "How did you do that?"

Nicole shrugged her shoulders and smiled. "I dared them to be quiet, sort of." She paused, then added, "You just have to turn it into a game."

I am learning. I am learning.

February, 2009

In the bleak mid-winter...

...Only the constant promise of the sun rising earlier with each passing day makes the morning run at all pleasant and tolerable. The kids are antsy and getting on each other's nerves. There is bickering and gossiping and surliness among some of them, and some actual punching, and it isn't play. The darkness descending early in the afternoon doesn't help, either. It is one of those times when you need to use all your weapons. So I start to write them up. That contains the difficulties to a great extent. They really don't like being written up, and all it takes is one or two write-ups and the word gets around quickly. It is an unfortunate state of affairs, and probably due in large part to Cabin Fever, but we manage to muddle through, and the bus rolls on.

But there are some bright events. For one, unexpectedly, there is The Great Melt. A late January Thaw hits in early February, and for a few days the temperature hovers in the fifties at noon, before the earth remembers what it is supposed to do. The temperature plummets back down to where it's supposed to be, and that's that.

Then there is the sudden appearance of The Owl. Predators start their nests early so that their fledglings are ready to swoop when the songbirds and voles appear later in the year. So it is not so much of a surprise when we look out the kitchen window one evening and there in the dusk, sitting on a branch of a cherry tree, seemingly looking straight at us, is a great Barred Owl.

We hear the owl calling during the night. It is flying down the ravine in back of our house, searching for prey, calling to its mate. The wild hooting of a Barred Owl is extraordinary. It scares you and lifts your spirit at the same time.

And then the next afternoon, while I am waiting for Bus 9 to arrive at Underhill Central, I glance into the trees and there is the Barred Owl again; whether the same one or a different one I will never know. All I know is that the owls are out and hungry, and I don't know if they are an omen of a late winter or an early spring. I will leave that to the experts. Already, on February 2nd, Punxsutawney Phil has seen his shadow and thus predicted another six weeks of winter. We shall see.

Meanwhile, it is Valentine's Day. It is our anniversary. On February 14th, 1973, Joanie and I met in an elevator on 14th Street in Manhattan. We were going up to the same party. It was on the 14th Floor. When we arrived there, the host introduced us. It has been quite a trip since then, and so we celebrate.

School let out on the afternoon of Friday the 20th, and immediately Joanie and I jumped into the car and headed south. It is the beginning of a school break that will last until March 3rd , Town Meeting Day—a welcome, long break from school bus duties. But we have a sad duty to perform. Saturday the 21st has been scheduled for Shelley's memorial service down in New Jersey, and so that is our destination. We drive through snowstorms to Saratoga, where we spend the night and get an early start the next morning, arriving in New Jersey just before the service is about to begin. The church is packed with people. Some of them we know; some we have never seen before.

Friends are invited to speak. Shelley's supervisor during her time as an Assistant District Attorney brings her original letter of hire signed by Robert Morganthau. Other co-workers from the DA's office speak. Shelley had the body of a ballerina, but she could be one tough cookie when she had to be. One of the ADA responsibilities during her time there was to take night duty. When there was a murder in the city after midnight, the ADA had to accompany the police to the crime scene. It was hard to imagine Shelley out on the dark streets in the middle of some of the worst neighborhoods in the city, examining crime scenes, interviewing suspects, and gazing at dead bodies, but she did it.

Friends from high school and college were there; friends from offices where she had worked; friends from college and law school. Four of her doctors were there, and they invariably spoke of her courage, and they meant it. They spoke from the heart. Her lead physician spoke a moving tribute to her that went to the essence of our friend.

Joanie read from a book of memories we had put together, and then presented the book to Shelly's daughter. Shelley's favorite songs were sung, a reception was held in the basement of the church, and we walked out into a beautiful spring-like day. But sadness hovered about the streets of that little surburban town.

We drove over to New York, where we had reserved a room at the Beekman Tower Hotel for a few nights. The Beekman is an older, Art Deco-style hotel at 49th Street and 1st Avenue, but what it lacks in modernity it makes up for in style. It's a suite hotel, which is handy in mid-Manhattan, because you have a small kitchen, and you can stock up at the little deli across the street and have your breakfasts in the comfort and quiet of your own digs. And you can pick up take-out at a couple of really good Chinese restaurants just a few blocks away. All of this is handy in a town where breakfast can run fifty bucks for two.

But of course we didn't eat in all the time. We met our

friend Dennis and went up to Melon's on 74th and 3rd for lunch on Sunday. Melon's is an old Irish neighborhood tavern that specializes in hamburgers. You can get a really good hamburger at Melon's for $8.95, which the natives seem to think is a great deal. It sure is a good hamburger. You may have to wait at the door for twenty or thirty minutes to be seated, but it's worth it. It's a lot of fun, too. Melon's has been written up in gourmet columns in Italy and Brazil, and it's sometimes full of Italians and Brazilians who have to eat there so they can go home and tell everybody they ate at Melon's. It's full of Upper East Siders, too, and you may find yourself seated next to somebody named Kennedy. Whatever, it's an uproarious, convivial spot. Highly recommended.

And of course we didn't stay stuck in our suite all the time. We went to the museums and movies and the ballet and all, but Sunday night we did stay in. Dennis brought some food in from places around town that he knew about, like this little place in the Village that specializes in breads and some dishes from the Shun Lee Dynasty, and we watched the Oscars.

Part of the Beekman deal was a complementary cocktail at their restaurant, so on Monday evening we took the elevator up to the twenty-sixth floor. That is the top floor. You walk out of the elevator into the restaurant's 1930s architecture and décor, and then you are led out to the edge of the building where you're seated at a table overlooking mid-town Manhattan. There is nothing much like that view anywhere else in the world.

As the night comes on, and the shadows fall across the streets below, the lights of Manhattan begin to glow. You sit and sip your wine and stare at the magnificent panorama that is beyond any exhibit at any art gallery or museum in the world. It is the sun and the moon and the stars. It is the galaxy carved and assembled anew and lit to perfection. Meanwhile, far below, the ghosts of Irving Berlin, Garbo, Dietrich, Bogart and Bergman glide through the purple shadows of the streets of Sutton Place, watched over by this symbol of the Deco Thirties.

You can sit there for hours and gaze and dream if this is a slow night. But this is Manhattan, and so there is never a slow night, and eventually you have to leave your table. And eventually, you have to leave Manhattan and go home, which we did. But I would be remiss if I didn't recommend The Beekman Tower to you. It's a good deal in February, when they run specials. In summer, watch out—it joins the rest of the merry throng of Manhattan hotels which can empty your wallets faster than you can say "derivative."

And so we came back to the hills of Underhill, and used the rest of the vacation to rest up and feed the fire and look out at the winter still swirling around, and it was as magical in its wintry way as New Jersey was spring-like or Manhattan was mighty and majestic. Part of this leisure time I used to contemplate how best I could improve my driving. I decided to attempt to define the perfect run, and here's what I came up with:

To make the perfect run you must be constantly alert. You must be focused on your immediate environment. You must prepare the bus correctly, examine all its systems and check for all possible defects. There must be no defects. When you begin to drive, you must compress your whole existence into what you see before you, to your sides, to your back. Your mind must not wander. You must not think of anything else. You must note every student waiting for you along your route. You must stop for each in an appropriate manner and guide the student onto the bus, taking care that every step of the way you have provided safety. You must remain on schedule. You cannot miss any stops, either when picking up students or dropping them off. You must be patient, both with the movement of the bus and the behavior of the students. You must guide the students into their right paths, and not allow them to stray out of bounds. They will test you, as they test their teachers and parents and society as a whole, for that is the job of a student—to test the boundaries.

You must be aware of what to see; what to look at; what to look for. You must be aware of the dangers: in the winter of ice; in the summer of heat; at all times of wind and rain and terrible drivers and distracted drivers and emergency situations and railroad crossings and intersections and falling branches and surprises of any kind around the next curve. You must be at one with the road. You must be constantly alert and able to see what other drivers do not see.

When you have simultaneously and constantly achieved all of these things, you will have achieved the Arrow of Zen. You will have made the Perfect Run.

Do you remember the magnificent beginning of the Kung Fu television show, where the blind master asks the boy, "Do you hear your own heartbeat? Do you hear the grasshopper which is at your feet?"

After the boy concedes that he does not, he in turn asks the master: "Old Man, how is it that you hear these things?"

The Master responds with a question: "Young man, how is it that you do not?"

When you hear and see everything around you, and you can concentrate fully and constantly, you will have the Perfect Run. You will have become the Arrow of Zen.

March, 2009

March is a strange month. It begins with Town Meeting Day, and there's a snap to the air that signals the onset of snow. Talk at the meeting is all about the weather, because the sap isn't running yet, and it should be; or it has been running, and all of a sudden it isn't; or it started too early; or what the blazes is going on, is there going to be a syrup season this year or isn't there?

This is the month when the signs appear:

"River In Flood"
"Beware Of Mud"
"Frost Heaves"
I'll bet he does,
When he perceives
Poems such as these...

March brings winds that rip the trees down. Major limbs fall over the roads, and you come around a bend and there's the end of the road, for the time being at least, until the road crew can get out and clear a path. And so you have opportunities, as some people like to say. You can call in and report the blockage. You can try to get around another way. You can just wait. But not with a bus full of kids.

March brings snow when you don't expect it and sunny days when you don't think you'll ever see the sun again. It brings rain. It brings hail and mud and grit, and you can't keep a car or a bus clean for more than a day at a time. At the end of some days, you wonder—what the blazes was that? The buses are wallowing through the mud. Roads are closed. Emergency construction pops up on your route where and when you least expect it. Schools devise special sessions and schedules and neglect to tell the transportation department about them. The kids are wild and crazy one Tuesday, with no explanation at all, until you look at the calendar and realize that it's a full moon.

And March goes on interminably. It stretches without a break for all its long weeks. The month is at least seven weeks long, because psychologically March doesn't end until the last week of April. It is a grueling stretch. Interminable. You are deep in the heart of the school year. Football is ended. Baseball hasn't begun. Hockey, that game built out of ice and cold and long winters under the northern lights, rules.

On television, there is March Madness, which is interminable in its own awful way, made tolerable only by the forecasts, which are always wrong. Are the forecasts part of the game? Are they there to make it more exciting? This is what goes through your mind on those dark winter nights while the cold is busy re-freezing the roads that the sun unfroze during the day, creating potholes that have no bottom to them known to man.

But—all this mad month you can smell springtime in the air. You can tell it's coming. The rivers and brooks are throwing off their winter coats. Animal tracks appear. The luge trails left behind on the river banks by otters tell the world that they're on the move once again. As you drive by the fields covered with melting snow, you see the tracks of mice and voles, of fisher and fox and coyote. You see the impress of wings where some great bird has swooped down on a hapless victim and snatched it into the air. And every morning, the sun rises a little bit earlier. It is inexorable in its climb up to the spring equinox and beyond. It is the only thing that keeps this month going, other than St. Patrick's Day. For suddenly, it is St. Patrick's Day, the anniversary of the Bear-Stearns meltdown, the anniversary of the decision that led ultimately to my driving this bus. And I still like it.

I like the kids. I like seeing them every morning. I like seeing them change and grow. I like their silliness and their grand funks and their interactions. I like watching them form bonds; form society. Society is being forged on this bus every day. The afternoon run home is like a decompression chamber for them. They get to interact in a way that they cannot during the school day or when they get home. And since spring is in the air, they do interact. Oh, yes. There is this thing called attraction. It affects people, whether they are in pre-school and hugging innocently; or in second grade and gazing into each other's eyes without knowing why; or punching each other as hard as possible in the middle grades; or falling in first and true love in high school; or holding hands after dinner in the retirement home. Ah, yes, attraction is at work, and spring is just around the corner, and like the old Irish song says:

> I'll tell my ma when I get home,
> The boys won't leave the girls alone;
> They pull my hair and they stole my comb,
> But that's all right till I go home.
>
> > She is handsome, she is pretty,
> > She is the belle of Belfast City;
> > She is a'courtin' one two three
> > Please won't you tell me who is she?
>
> Albert Mooney says he loves her,
> All the boys are fightin' for her;
> Knocking the door, ringing the bell,
> Saying oh my true love, are you well?

Out she comes then bright as snow,
Rings on her fingers, bells on her toes;
Old Johnny Morrissey says she'll die
If she doesn't get the fella with the rovin' eye.

Let the wind and the rain and the hail blow high
And the snow come whistlin' through the sky;
She's as nice as apple pie and
She'll get her own lad by and by.

When she gets a lad of her own
She won't tell her ma when she gets home;
Let them all come as they will
For it's Albert Mooney she loves still.

> I'll tell my ma when I get home
> The boys won't leave the girls alone
> They pull my hair and they stole my comb
> But that's all right till I go home...

Enough said on that subject. The old song says it better than I ever could. I will just note the fact that life goes on, with all its joys and heartaches, at whatever age. Beyond that, let us leave these growing, vibrant young humans with their privacy intact. I would not like them to tell on me; and I will not tell on them. Besides, they all sit in back of me, if you get my drift.

And so I will observe their shenanigans, whether caused by attraction or by any of the other appetites we as a race are subject to, and I will simply smile and hum my old song and be happy. Life is good.

But always still, there is the threat of something going amiss. All through the winter, drivers asked me how Irish Settlement Road was holding up. Irish Settlement had a reputation: a reputation for breaking up; a reputation for closing down. Bob and Julia Northrop, who live up there, told me about conditions way back in the sixties when most of the land was still in farming, and fields instead of forests stretched all along the length of the road. "There were years," said Bob, "when the snow was piled so high in the road—sometimes six feet or more—that a bus driver would just take to the fields. See, the wind would whip all the snow off the fields and deposit it in the roadbed, but the ground had frozen, so it was just a natural thing to do. To get up Flynn Hill, say, a driver would just veer off the road at the bottom, drive up through the fields, and get back on the road at the top of the hill. Made for an exciting ride. Wasn't dangerous or anything."

"The kids *loved* it," Julia said.

So we were all waiting for Irish Settlement Road to do something, but it hadn't. I had driven it enough before my bus-driving days to experience some of what it could do, but for some reason, this year it had done nothing. Still, I was wary. I was aware of its disposition and its propensities, and I was of the belief that it was just biding its time and plotting some outrage.

April, 2009

Wednesday, April 8, 2009
The Cruelest Day

April has been called the cruelest month. That's not necessarily so, but let me tell you about the cruelest day in April, 2009, in Underhill, Vermont. Everybody has 'off' days, but I would say that entire days have 'off' days, too, and whatever you do to offset that might or might not work.

April 8th was like that. It began with a coldness in the air that was more like March than May. There was a steel-gray overcast that had not been predicted. At about 6:50 AM it started to snow, and by 7 AM there was an inch on the ground. I started my run up Pleasant Valley being very careful. The plows had not been out. No sanding or salting had been done. Nobody had expected this. The snow did not appear to be extraordinarily slippery; still, caution was indicated.

I turned left onto Irish Settlement Road, picking up kids as usual. Everything seemed fine. In front of Kimberly's house there was a bit of snow build-up, and the bus slipped a little as I braked. Another sign to be cautious, I said to myself. And I was. I made my way farther along the road, picking up kids all the way. The snow disappeared in places; reappeared in others. By the time I was making my approach to the hill by Donovan Road, the snow had appeared again, with pretty good coverage here.

I decided that after I picked up the Donovan kids, I would repeat what I had been doing all winter long—that is, I would load them, then back up a few hundred feet and give the bus a good head of steam so the momentum would carry it to the top of the hill. I didn't care that it was almost spring. These were winter conditions, and a winter driving response was warranted.

I spotted the Donovans waiting by the left side of the road, which seemed to be covered by about an inch or two of snow. I slowed and put on the ambers. I took up the center of the road, right on the crown, and applied the brakes. The bus stopped. I was about to put on the reds. Ryan and Claire were leaning forward, ready to cross the road. And suddenly, from a standing stop, the bus began to move. It slid back and sideways, right off the middle of the road. I took my foot off the brake. It slid. I took it out of gear. It slid. I tried reverse gear, trying to change its course. No such luck. I tried braking again. It slid to the side of the road.

When it reached the side of the road, I tried to bring it forward, using the same method I had used in the fall. That didn't work, either. The right front wheel slid off into the deepest part of the drainage ditch, right over the culvert where it was about three feet deep. The whole bus pitched over, leaning sideways at about a 35-degree angle. You have to understand that this all happened in slow motion. It was like being on a glacier that was moving down a mountainside. It was incredible. My feeling of helplessness was complete. I watched the mirrors on the passenger side of the bus come to rest on the hillside beyond the ditch. Even as the kids in the back of the bus were yelling "Hey! You're sliding into a tree!" the bus came to a halt. Not a screeching halt. Not a jarring halt. Just a nice, easy, ho-hum, here-we-are halt. Nothing wrong at all, except I suddenly had the responsibility for over forty kids and a bus leaning over at a 35-degree angle on its side in a ditch on a really cold day, and I had to turn off the engine, which meant no heat.

I switched off the engine, turned on the four-ways, and got up and looked down the length of the bus. "Okay," I said. "It doesn't look like we are going anywhere anytime soon. I need everybody to keep calm, and Chris and Chuck and Ben, I need you guys to help get everybody out of the back door. Just like a drill, okay? Not yet, but when another bus gets to us. I'll go first, then you follow me out. Be ready, okay?" They nodded their heads.

A few of the kindergartners began to whimper and cry. All of a sudden, Deidre stood up in the middle of the bus, pointed to her little brothers and sister, and said loudly, "You, you, and you. You are mine. I don't want to hear anything out of you. Is that clear? Not a word. Not a peep. Now listen..." And before you knew it, she had gathered them and the other little ones around her and she was telling them a story. And they were listening, and calming down. And so was I. Sort of.

I got on the radio and called Base. No answer. I called again. Still nothing. A neighbor appeared at my window and offered a cell phone. Just as she did so, Base answered. A lot of static, but we were getting through to each other. Holly was on the other end. I reported the details to her. She relayed to Bob Magee, and he immediately sent out Doug in a rescue bus. Bob wanted to know if there was any smell of fuel in the bus. I checked. The fuel tank was intact. Good.

I thanked the neighbor and assured Base that there was no immediate danger. We considered the weather, the conditions, the fact of the soft landing, and the decision was made to keep the kids in the bus until another bus arrived. It would be a while. I advised Doug to travel up Pleasant Valley Road to the second entrance to Irish Settlement and come down from the north to us instead of trying to come up from the south. The southern approach would have been closer, but it would have entailed his trying to come down Flynn Hill, which had already

put me into the ditch. All I could think of was watching a bus losing traction and careening down the hill onto us. No sense dealing with a nightmare scenario like that. So I told him to come from the north. He agreed, and I breathed easier.

When I got off the radio, I surveyed the interior of the bus. The little ones were still gathered around Deidre. The others were sitting quietly or talking in small groups. "Listen up," I said. "There's another bus coming to get us, but it will be a while. He'll be coming to us from the north entrance. He'll be stopping a ways back, by the Kelleys' driveway, so he doesn't get into the same mess we're in. I'm just asking you to be patient and calm, okay? When the bus gets here, we'll go out the back door. Then we will walk down the road directly to the other bus. Any questions?"

"When will the other bus get here?" somebody asked.

"It will be a while," I said, "but I'll let you know. I'll be on the radio with him, and I'll let you know exactly where he is. I'll call him every few minutes until he gets here."

"It better be quick," said a middle school student. "I can miss my Language Arts class, but I've got a math test second period. Gotta be there."

"We'll see," I said.

"It's déjà vu all over again," said Deidre. I must have looked puzzled.

"It usually goes off the road at the *top* of the hill," Nicole chimed in.

I let that remark go. At that point, I didn't want to know this little piece of history. I had enough to think about as it was.

We sat down to wait. Every few minutes, I would call Doug, and he would report his progress. On Pleasant Valley Road. At Corbett's Corners. Turning into Irish Settlement. At Conklin Road intersection. At Doon Road intersection.

When Doug reported arriving at Doon Road, I stood up and said: "The other bus will be here in a few minutes. It's time to get ready to leave. Now, listen carefully. Like I said before, we'll go out the back door. I will go first. I will go out and wait until I see Bus 8 at Kelley's driveway. Then, Cal and Chris and Chuck will begin to move everybody out. Move slowly. Be very careful, especially when you are going out the door and dropping to the ground. Everybody's okay now. Let's keep it that way."

Before I could move toward the back, Nicole came up the aisle. "Can I be Sweep? I wanna be Sweep!"

"Sure you can," I said. Good thought. Always good to have a sweep.

I went down the aisle, past kid after kid waiting to go out. Strange feeling. I got to the back and looked at the guys assigned to help to see that they were ready. They were. I opened the back door, sat down on the floor of the bus, and dropped out. Whoa!

I hit the snow and it wasn't snow. It was ice. Pure ice. So that's what had happened. Just in this one spot over the length of this road, conditions were such that it wasn't a snowfall but an icefall, if there is any such thing. Whatever it was, I went skittering away across the ice, trying to keep to my feet. I must have skidded down that road ten feet before I could stop. It was like standing on a slanted hockey rink. The guys at the back of the bus thought it was a riot. There they were, standing at the door, laughing their heads off.

I got back to the bus and turned and looked down the road. Doug was just pulling Bus 8 to a stop at Kelley's. I looked up at my assistants and said, "Okay, guys. Come on down. But don't jump standing up. Sit down and just jump off from there."

So, of course, Chuck jumped from a standing position. Off he went, skating down the road. "Yowee!" he yelled.

Since Chuck had jumped, Calvin had to jump. Since Calvin had jumped, Chris had to jump. No question; just something they had to do. So there were the three of them, zipping along the ice, laughing and having a great old time.

That didn't last long. They got themselves together, got back to the door, and suddenly became really mature and competent. They were terrific. They helped each of the other kids down, and a ragged line formed and headed for Doug's bus. All the kids were great. They all did exactly as they were told. Well, all but Deidre, who said "What do you mean, sit down? I'll get my jeans wet." But then she did sit down, and they took her arms to steady her and she hopped out and walked gingerly down the ice.

Last to come out was Nicole, as Sweep, holding a yowling kindergartner in her arms. The kindergartner had decided that staying in the bus was preferable to going out into the unknown. Can't say as I blame him, but he didn't stand a chance with Nicole. She picked him up out of his seat, pried his hands off their handholds, and marched him on down the aisle in her arms, him howling all the way. She handed him down to the guys, and then came down herself, and that was that. I closed the door and started for Bus 8.

SCHOOL BUS
SYRUP

I cannot begin to tell you how good those kids were in that emergency. Looking back at it, I still find it hard to believe. They were extraordinary; all of them. There is nothing more to be said about it.

The bus ride back to the schools was uneventful. Doug drove cautiously and slowly. We dropped off the elementary kids first, then the middle schoolers, then the high schoolers. Then I thanked Doug and went to the bus garage. Earl was just about to take a small bus out to Bus 4. I asked to go with him. "Come on aboard," he said. He explained that they would try to pull Phil out of the ditch with this one. "I don't know about that," I said. "Well, we'll see," said Earl.

When Earl and I arrived at the site of the accident, Bob was already there. "Don't even bother calling the local guy," he said to Earl. "Call Burlington and get their biggest tow truck out here."

Earl drove back to the garage, where Jon and Roger had another bus ready for me. I got in and drove it back to Underhill Center. I parked it and went home, had lunch, and then I was ready for the afternoon run.

Well, that afternoon run was another story, let me tell you. There we were, seven buses in a circle waiting for dismissal of classes at Jericho Elementary School when the first announcement came over the radios. It was Holly, calling from Base: "All drivers who are scheduled to arrive at Brown's River Middle School this afternoon, listen carefully. Do not go to Brown's River. We will let you know where to go in a few minutes, but again, do not attempt to go to Brown's River. There is an incident in progress. Do not go to Brown's River."

A reply from a driver at the ID Elementary School, which shared a campus with Brown's River: "We're at the ID, and we're loading already. Then we're supposed to go over to Brown's River. What do you want us to do?"

"Finish loading and sit tight."

Holly was back within two minutes. "Okay. Everyone. Here's what you do. Do not, I repeat, do not go anywhere near Brown's River. If you are scheduled to go there, drive over to Villeneuve's Lumber and park over there. Go into the yard from the Route 15 side. Line up and stay there. Wait for further instructions. ID drivers, circle out of the area and go over to Villeneuve's, also. We will let you know when it is time to proceed to Brown's River. Sit tight until you hear from us. Ten-four."

So, an incident at Brown's River. What could it be? I loaded up some 25 Jericho students and dropped them at their homes, then proceeded toward Brown's River. Where the River Road forked off from Route 15 towards the schools, I continued on Route 15 until, in a few hundred yards, I came to Villeneuve's. There I lined up behind the buses that were already parked, and we waited.

Through the bare tree branches, we could see the flashing blue lights of the State Police patrol cars. We could see fire trucks. We caught snatches of rumors. We waited a long time. Some of the buses had a lot of kids in them, and they began to get squirmy. I was glad I had an empty bus. Then parents appeared among the buses, searching for their kids. They'd been alerted by the ID school—instructions on where to find them. As kids were taken off one by one, two by two, family by family, we sat. We were there well over an hour.

It was a bomb scare. I hesitate to call it a prank. I don't call it a prank. It goes over the line. Bomb scares in schools are more common than you think, mainly perpetrated by a kid (or kids) who have, for whatever reason, gone temporarily insane. For some reason, they feel like the threat can get them out of a test, or out of school, or scare the daylights out of the authorities. All of the above reasons are true in the sense that it works, temporarily. Usually the kid thinks it's funny, but in the era of Columbine and 9/11, it is anything but funny, and each incident has to be taken as seriously as possible. Still, they do it. I suppose, to be most generous to the little squirrel-heads, it is an outlawed part of the testing of society that teens and preteens and, let's face it, adults do all the time. It stinks. And it goes on all over, constantly.

This time, it was a piece of paper left in a bathroom. On the paper was one word: Bomb. That was enough to shut down the school, call in the police, evacuate the building (they brought everybody over to the ID school), interrogate each kid, keep everybody in turmoil for two hours, and disrupt the day for everybody in the community.

The result was that I picked up a bunch of exhausted middle schoolers at Brown's River. By the time I got out to Underhill Central to pick up the elementary kids, there were none left. They had all been picked up by parents or designated neighbors and friends. I dropped off the middle schoolers and high schoolers and went home.

But April 8th wasn't finished with us yet. When we turned on the TV news that night we heard that a Vermont man was being held hostage by Somali pirates. Richard Phillips of Underhill was the captain of a shipping vessel that was on its way to Africa with food and other aid when his ship was attacked, and now he was a prisoner of Somali pirates.

April 8th was one hell of a day in Underhill.

Richard and Andrea Phillips had a house on River Road, the main road leading into Underhill Center. It's a beautiful old traditional white farmhouse with a white picket fence in front of it and a couple of red barns across the road. It's surrounded by pasture and forest and land that slopes gently away and down to Brown's River. It is made to order for the media, and by the next morning, April 9th, when we went by on the bus at 7:40 AM, the media had already begun to gather. There were perhaps ten or so reporters across the road from the house, and more were arriving by the second. One of those big transmitting trucks with a huge white disk on top was in place behind the barn. Someone had already tied yellow ribbons to the picket fence. I slowed, and the kids took a look at the house and the media people.

I had already dropped off the elementary kids, so all the students on the bus were either middle or high schoolers. They were silent as we passed the house, but boy, were they ever alert. They took everything in as we passed.

I dropped them at the school and turned back down River Road to park the bus. By the time I passed the Phillips house again, the reporters had crossed the road and were hanging over the picket fence.

Within the hour, the reporters were back on the opposite side of the street, gently herded over there by Vermont State Police. The Governor had called Andrea Phillips and asked if there was anything he could do. "Send me some troopers and get these reporters off my fence before they break it," she said. The troopers arrived and moved the reporter scrum back across the street.

By 3 PM, when we passed again, there were at least a half-dozen media disk trucks wth cameras and reporters of all kinds in evidence. The trucks were parked in the field behind the barns. The reporters were planted three deep on one side of the road, all looking intently at the house on the other side. Richard Phillips was half a world away, adrift in a lifeboat with four Somali pirates, and this was as close as the reporters could get to him.

On Friday, Captain Phillips jumped out of the lifeboat and began swimming toward the USS Bainbridge, which had shown up along with the USS Boxer to try to rescue him. The pirates went in after him and retrieved him. By Friday, also, the troopers had moved the reporters and their paraphernalia a mile down the road into the center of town, where the communica-

tions trucks—nine of them by this time—parked themselves in the St. Thomas parking lot and across from the Town Hall. The reporters fanned out all over downtown Underhill Center—all two blocks of it—and started interviewing pedestrians, all they could corner. All three of them. Then they went on to interview each other.

They commented on the town. They stated that it was an agricultural community located ten minutes from Burlington International Airport.

The only way it could meet that description was if the reporters had flown in from the airport in a Cessna and landed in a field off River Road and immediately stepped in some farm output, all of which was unlikely. We were good-humored about their mistakes. Most likely they were just pretty bleary by Friday. Interviewed by townsfolk, the reporters revealed that they worked in twelve-hour shifts. They were quartered at The Inn at Essex, about a dozen miles down the road toward Burlington, so we didn't feel too sorry for them. We saved our sadness for the Phillips family. By Friday, the yellow ribbons reached the entire length of River Road and beyond. They were on every pole and fence and tree of any size alongside the road. There were flowers left at the Phillips house. People brought them and then immediately left Andrea and her family to their privacy.

But you could understand why the reporters might think we were an agricultural community. As you cross the Underhill town line, you can gaze down the valley almost to Underhill Center. As you drive along the River Road, you pass fields and farmhouses and barns and chickens and sheep and places to buy eggs and Chamberlin's Produce Stand and *a lot* of open space. You will count 21 barns along that three-mile stretch of road. They are not all classic barns. Some are. The old white Fay barn is stunning. There are traditional red barns of varied shape and size. There are old pole barns and modern vinyl-sided barns, some of them only a couple of years old. The last one built was for the Sullivans, to replace an older barn that burned. And you know, it was built by local guys. All of a sudden, one day there were scores of pick-ups and trucks in the Sullivan field, and guys were scampering all over the place, and walls were going up, and carpenters were standing on the top level and placing trusses, and you knew these guys. They were your neighbors and friends, and they were having an old-fashioned barn-raising right there in the middle of our town. So yeah, I suppose you might think of Underhill as a rural agricultural community.

But ten minutes from Burlington airport? Not very likely. Never heard of anybody doing it that fast. Still, that's what the CNN lady was still reporting on Saturday night from the parking lot across the street from Town Hall. It was 9:00 PM, getting pretty dark, but still enough light to see the Town Hall across the street. She was using it for a backdrop for her report. The wind was blowing and her hair kept blowing across her face and microphone, and these cute little snowflakes were dancing across her eyes, and she was reporting that the street was almost deserted, and she figured that the weather was so bad that it had driven people into their homes early this wintry night.

She was wrong on a number of counts. First, 9:00 PM isn't early in Underhill. It's when a lot of people are already in bed and most of the others are almost there. The Saturday evening Mass at St. Thomas' was over and those people were gone. The Country Store was closed. So was Wells' Market. The only normal reason to be there would be to walk your dog, and not too many people were doing that this night. The only other reason would be to take pictures of the reporters and their trucks (which had taken on the flavor of a local sport); and true, the light was not the best for that at this time of night.

As for the weather, it was a pleasant spring evening in Underhill, what with the snow coming down gently, a nice breeze blowing and the temperature at 30 degrees.

WNCD

The other factor was that it was Holy Saturday, and a lot of people were busy at home preparing for Easter Sunday festivities: laying out clothes for church; laying out snowshoes and skis for the Easter Sunrise service on top of Mt. Mansfield; laying out chocolate and colored eggs; getting ready for guests; getting ready to be guests—all that sort of thing.

Yes, tomorrow would be Easter Sunday, and that too was a factor in the traffic pattern in downtown Underhill Center that wintry night.

And what an Easter Sunday it was, for when we woke and turned on the radios and TVs, the biggest news of the day was that Richard Phillips was Free. Alive. Well. What a day!

Yellow ribbons and Mobile Units were still all over Underhill Center. CNN was still in the Town Hall parking lot. Fox44 parked at Chamberlin's farm. The rest clustered at the Phillips home. And they all helped us celebrate as a town and as a nation. And then, without warning, they were gone, leaving us again to our own devices.

Another miracle. First Sully Sullenberger planting that jet in the Hudson; now Richard Phillips freed from the pirates. What would come next? Was this to be a year of miracles? Was this to be a year of soft water landings? Who knew? All we knew was, there was hope for the future if this kind of thing kept happening.

So what else happened in April? What about the bus? What happened to the bus?

On Wednesday, the day after the ice incident, Courtney got onto the substitute bus during the morning run and looked at me and said, "Is the bus alright?"

Yes, Courtney, the bus was alright. They had hitched it up and pulled it out of the ditch. There was not a scratch on it. It had been such a soft landing that there was not even a single scratch. They towed it over to the garage and inspected it carefully. They looked it over and tested it for two days. They were even more thorough than usual in their inspection. The bus was fine. By Friday, Phil was back in business.

May, 2009

So Chris gets onto the bus one morning and stands right in front of me and looks at me, and I look back at him, and he holds up two quarters and puts them over his eyes and says, "Look! I've been quarter-eyezed!"

SOMETHING'S OUT THERE.

Maybe it was some kind of hangover from the ice/bomb/Captain Phillips day, but as the year came to a close, I couldn't help but feel that something was out there, waiting to do mischief or even something more drastic.

Something was out there, around the next bend, waiting to happen. As a result, I became ever more vigilant when driving. I became more cautious. When turning, I would not gauge the speed of an approaching vehicle and judge if it were safe enough to turn into traffic or not. I would wait. I would take no chances.

Maybe it was the memory of that April day, or maybe it was something else. Maybe it was the mailbox incident, or the Preston Ponds incident, both of which occurred in May.

The month of May was crammed with field trips. The world was warming up to summer, the kids were getting restless with the knowledge that school's end was right around the corner, and there were plenty of opportunities to get them out of the classroom and into the world. The buses were kept full and busy all day long.

So on one day I found myself at 8:30 AM in front of Jericho Elementary School waiting for a busload of third graders and their teachers and chaperones/parents to board for a trip to Preston Ponds, up in the cliffs of Bolton. The kids came on, each with a backpack full of lunch and an observation notebook and a water bottle and whatever. Then came the science teachers carrying insect nets for capturing and showing dragonflies and tadpoles and frog eggs and water-beetle larvae and whatever else was buzzing or croaking or oozing around up there in the ponds. Then came at least a half-dozen parents, looking a bit uncomfortable and tentative and wondering how they got into this in the first place.

The sun was shining. The temperature was climbing toward eighty, but there was still a tingle of springtime in the air. The windows and roof hatches were all open, and everybody relaxed as I pulled out of the school yard and swung onto Route 15. I made my way to Brown's Trace and took it through Jericho Center, then turned left onto Nashville Road and headed for the hills. Halfway to West Bolton, I stopped so everyone could look at Snowflake Bentley's home, a big old Victorian set on pleasant, mature tree-and-garden acreage.

It was entirely appropriate to stop there. We were on a science trip, after all, and Snowflake Bentley was Jericho's earliest scientist. Bentley was the first person, back in the 19th century, to photograph snowflakes. Up close. Up really close. Close enough to discover that no two snowflakes were alike. Year after year, Bentley photographed thousands upon thousands of snowflakes, enough to astonish both the scientific and general populations. His work became one of the building blocks of modern scientific advancements. His work led others to consider more deeply the nature of atoms. Today, his picture is on display in a place of honor in the Jericho Town Hall. There are books about him for sale in the Old Red Mill gift shop next to the world-famous Joe's Snack Bar on Route 15, across from Laurie's Mane Street beauty salon. There are snowflake earrings there, too; and snowflake pendants, snowflake necklaces, snowflake Christmas ornaments, snowflake tee shirts, and snowflake anything else that can incorporate snowflakes. Yes, Bentley is well-remembered in Jericho. So we stopped for a minute while one of the teachers explained Snowflake's history to the kids.

Then we went on, easterly, ever easterly. Past the farms, past the West Bolton Golf Club, through the town of West Bolton itself, stopping at the stop sign on the corner. Then up Stage Road to a sharp left turn onto Notch Road, then up past some stunning cliffs to the Preston Ponds trailhead. Here I left them. I would pick them up at 1 PM over at another trailhead on Stage Road, which I would have to find later. I drove down Notch Road a considerable ways to a turnaround, past the Long Trail crossing point, and by the time I passed by again, there was no sign of them at all. They had all disappeared into the woods—kids, parents, teachers, the whole kit and caboodle of them. I silently wished them well and drove back to Underhill.

I arrived at the trailhead on Stage Road at 12:40, and I was surprised to see that a few of the kids were already waiting by the side of the road. I found a good shaded spot to park (the temperature was nearly ninety by that time), turned off the bus, opened the door, and waited. I could hear the shouts and calls of the others as they came down the trail. Soon everybody was aboard, all steamy and overheated. The nets of the science teachers were slimy with pond junk. The kids were hot, and wanted nothing more than for the bus to start so a breeze, however oven-like, could give them at least a breath of fresh air.

It was one o'clock. That was fine with me. No lost kids; everybody reasonably happy; plenty of time to get them back to Jericho in time for the afternoon run. I closed the doors and turned on the ignition. Nothing happened. I ran the shift lever through the gears. Sometimes if the lever wasn't in the exact position, the engine wouldn't turn over. No, that wasn't it. I ran through the routine of things that could be wrong. I checked the lever for the door's air system to make sure it was correctly locked in. I walked to the back of the bus and checked the rear emergency door lock. A buzzer should have gone off if the door was open. It hadn't, but I wanted to check anyway. I fiddled with the lock mechanism, to make sure it was catching correctly. I walked back up through the bus (murmurs of "What's wrong? What's he doing? Why aren't we going?" trailing behind me like some kind of ghostly mantra.) I checked all the emergency-window lock levers. I shut and opened the overhead hatches. Nothing wrong there.

Two of the teachers had driven buses of one kind or an other during their careers, and they offered suggestions. I checked the battery gauge—that was okay. Everything was okay, except that the bus wouldn't start. Had I done something? Wrong? Stupid? Ignorant? Questions like that go through your mind at times like this.

I finally gave up and called in. Thankfully the radio still worked. Holly answered in the office. I told her my predicament and she began to go through the litany of things to check, all of which I had already checked except for the last: "Do you have any fuel in the tank?" That startled me for the second it took to glance at the fuel gauge. But, yes, plenty of fuel. "Okay," Holly said. "Mechanic will be right out. Twenty minutes or so. Give me your location again."

It was a long twenty minutes. I don't know if it was longer for me or for the kids. They were really good, though, for finding themselves stuck out in the middle of nowhere in a hot bus with no end to their predicament in sight.

At about 1:30 Bob Magee's old truck appeared tootling down the road. It stopped and out hopped Bob. No mechanic, though. I wondered what Bob could do about this. Was a mechanic right behind him, possibly driving a spare bus?

I got out of the bus with a couple of the teachers as Bob approached. Before I could say anything, Bob checked to see that everyone was clear of the bus. Then he dove under the front wheels. He jiggled something under there and the engine roared to life. He came out from under and said, "Take it directly to Jericho Elementary. Be sure it doesn't stall. Get these kids back to school. Pull up in the circle, right in front of the door, like you usually do. Whatever you do, don't turn it off. Earl will be right behind you with a spare bus. Swap with Earl after you get the kids off. You should be in and out of there before anybody else arrives. You can circle around in the spare bus and get into your regular position. Remember, don't shut it off!" Then he was gone.

So finally we got started back to Jericho. I pulled into the circle, stopped at the front door of the school, threw the bus into neutral, pulled on the emergency brake, and shut off the engine. Then I sat there and stared at my hand, still on the key in the ignition.

It was all those months of training. It was all those warnings echoing through my mind, drummed into my brain, until I just did it automatically. "Never idle in a schoolyard," over and over and over again in meetings and reinforced every time you entered a school property. "They'll be watching, and they'll report you if you idle." "If parents complain because their kids are cold, tell them to change the law if they want to, but we'll obey it until they do."

I had done well, on one level. I had followed my training to a tee. On another level, I sat there wondering what had happened to my brain. Maybe it was the heat? I picked up the radio transmitter again and called in to the office. I told Holly what had happened.

"You did what?" she said. Then, "I'll get in touch with Bob." She did. Then I heard Bob contact Earl. "Bring a starter kit with you," he said. Meanwhile the other six buses were arriving and piling up in back of me. This was embarrassing. Every driver in the fleet was listening, I knew. I sat there in my empty, dead bus, and I started to laugh. I couldn't help it. I couldn't believe what I had done. Then Earl showed up and dove under the bus, just like Bob had done. Did they all know how to do this? The bus roared into life again. Earl, sweaty from his exertions, appeared in the doorway. "Okay," he said, "Pull it around. *Don't* turn it off again. If you turn it off again ..."

The lesson I took from this incident was this: there were gremlins around, and they were looking to create mischief. If I did anything even vaguely out of line, even just the tiniest bit over the line from standard operating procedure, they were going to find me. I would pay. Even finding out later that I had done nothing to cause the bus to falter, that it was a mechanical flaw, didn't make me feel better. I became even more cautious.

Two weeks later was the Mailbox Incident.

That morning, as I sat outside the ID School waiting to take a couple of classes down to the Echo Center on the Burlington waterfront, I caught a glimpse of Craig behind my bus. My first thought was that he was going on the same trip, but then I noticed he was driving one of the small vans. I wondered why he wasn't coming up to say hello. He seemed to be looking at something in the rear of the bus. I went out and found him examining the back of the bus really closely. As I approached, he turned to me and said, "Nothing to worry about. Just had to check on something. No problem here. Gotta go." And he went.

Strange, I thought, but basically shrugged my shoulders.

But the next day, after the morning run, Bob called me on the radio and asked me to come over to the garage as soon as possible. Now I knew by this time that it was never a good thing to be asked to "come over to the garage as soon as possible." I went immediately. Might as well get it over with, whatever it was.

When I walked into the office, Bob looked at me and said, "Hit a mailbox?"

My reply was eloquent. "Huh?"

"Did you hit a mailbox?"

"No, not that I remember. I would have reported it."

"Well, we've got to check it out. Somebody reported you hit a mailbox. He wants us to pay for it. Where's the bus?"

"Out in the line."

"Let's look at it." We left the office. Craig, Alan, and Earl were waiting outside. Earl had his bus condition report folder with him. The four of us walked out to old Phil. Bob, Alan, Craig, and Earl started at the front of the bus, worked their way down the passenger side, across the back, and up the other side back to the front, all of them closely scrutinizing every aspect of the bus. At one point Craig pointed to a small dent—I mean a *small* dent—way back on the passenger side and said, "What about this?"

Earl looked at the report folder. "No," he said. "That was from a fence, two-and-a-half years ago."

That was the only thing they could find that showed the least bit of evidence of contact with anything like a mailbox. There were no other dents, no scraped paint, nothing. But it wasn't that they didn't try to find anything. They gave it an inspection like the next thing they were going to do was call the troopers and have me locked up if they found anything.

"Looks okay," said Bob, and headed back to the garage with Earl.

"Let's go for a ride," said Craig.

"A ride? What for?"

"Practice backing up." He motioned me onto the bus. We got on and I started it up.

"Where do you want to go?" I asked.

"How about Old Pump Road?"

"Okay," I said. "Why Old Pump Road?"

"Practice backing up," said Craig, and was pretty much silent on the way over.

Now Old Pump Road was the first road I hit on the afternoon run out of Jericho. It was a winding, country, gravel road. I would go up it, dropping off eight or nine kids on the way; then, just before it crossed the town line from Jericho to Essex, I would turn around in a private driveway. This was done by a long-standing agreement with the owner. Then I would drive back down Old Pump Road to Route 15 and go on from there.

We turned onto Old Pump Road and I asked Craig where he wanted me to turn around.

"Where you usually turn around. Just do it the way you usually would do it. I just want to see how you do it."

"You mean that mailbox is the one everybody's talking about? I saw it was dinged. A couple of days ago. I didn't hit it."

"Well, just show me how you turn here."

We were coming up to the driveway. "I turn just like Alan showed me how at the beginning of the year." I pulled up to my mark. I turned exactly the same way every day. I would pull up to a spot on the road right across from a fork on the limb of a tree. I took up the whole of the narrow road, then backed into the driveway until the bus doors were right even with the mashed mailbox.

"Hey," said Craig, "that was pretty good. Pull out and do it again, will you?" He stood up and put the door lever into emergency position. Then he swung the doors open. I pulled out onto the road and started back into the driveway again. Craig, holding onto the bar on the stairway, poked his head out the door and watched.

"You're nowhere near that mailbox," he said.

"Want me to get closer?"

"No, that's okay..." but I was already back on the road. I pulled up farther than I usually would and cut the wheel and started back.

"Careful," said Craig, "you're near the ditch."

I knew that. I could see where I was through the back-up mirror. I had that bus right on the edge of the driveway. I pulled it all the way back again, and we looked at the offended mailbox. It was still a few feet away, on the other side of a steep drainage ditch.

"You couldn't have hit that mailbox," said Craig. He sounded relieved. "Look at it. It's down there in the weeds. The bus is too high to hit it. Somebody else hit it, and I'd say whoever hit it was coming the other way. That's good enough for me. Let's go back."

As we drove back down the road, Craig said, "Should've had the camera with me. That woulda clinched it. Well, if this thing keeps on going, we can always come back out with a camera. Nice driving."

"Thanks," I said. I meant it. I took two things away from this incident. First, it reinforced my belief that Bob protected his drivers and stood up for them. With this particular incident, of course, he had to be sure I was innocent before he acted. I was impressed by the attention the whole organization had paid. Bob had been out and inspected the mailbox. So had Craig. Then there was Craig's initial inspection of the bus, and then the inspection at the garage. I was really thankful for Earl's detailed and dated condition notes. And I was impressed by the depth and thoroughness of the investigation.

The homeowner wanted a mailbox to replace the damaged one, and he'd asked the district to pay for it. But Bob had his back up on this one, and I could see why. To pay for the box—what—$20? $25? —would be to admit that a district bus driver had done it. Simple enough to write a check and have the thing go away. But to admit that would be untrue, for one thing; and for another it would have meant that a driver had broken the rule that said everything got reported. That rule was what maintained the integrity of the outfit Bob had built. And beyond that, it would have opened the District to culpability in the incident. True, this was a seemingly small incident, but one of the most important things this outfit had going for it was its attention to detail—to the *smallest* detail. That was how to maintain a bus; how to discipline students; how to hone your skill to the greatest degree possible; how to face the day: pay attention and make sure it's right. Like I said: this was a great organization.

The other thing I took away from the incident was a deepening belief that there *was* something out there trying its best to ruin this year, even if there were only a few driving days left. And I was right about that. There was something out there trying hard to make life miserable. But it didn't get me. It got someone else, in a big way.

It got Bill.

"Clear the air!"

It was that terrible order coming through once more. Then there were only snatches of sentences. "Get your flares out." "Make up your seating chart. Make sure you know where all those kids were sitting..." "The troopers will be there in a minute..."

We couldn't hear any replies. The bus was way down south, out in the hills. Our radios wouldn't carry that far. We could hear the Base radio and what was said to the bus in trouble down there, but we couldn't pick up any return answers.

It was the afternoon run. Bill was stopped on a country road at a designated school bus stop. He had his brake on and his reds were flashing. He was letting a couple of kids off the bus. All of a sudden, something slammed into the back of the bus with enough force to drive the rear bumper a foot forward under the bus.

The car went that far under the bus too. A young woman was driving. She came up over the hill and didn't even see the bus. She was distractred.

Fortunately nobody was hurt. But it's that sort of thing that really wrecks you for a good long while. It drives home the importance of taking every precaution. Safety is primary. The responsibility of what you are engaged in is driven home with the force of a sledgehammer. It doesn't matter that nobody appeared to be hurt in this instance. The driver of the car was injured; so were the kids on the bus; so was the bus driver. The injury was not physical, perhaps. But the memory of the accident and what might have happened will stay with them all for a good long time. Maybe, in little flashes of memory down through the years, forever.

But we all got through the rest of May, and there were some great days during that month. One day there was magic in the air. While they were waiting for the older kids, the little girls on the afternoon Jericho run—the preschoolers and the kindygartners— turned themselves into princesses. Not willing to be a princess, Lucas transformed himself into a choo-choo. But he was right there to choo-choo along with the princesses. And the princesses needed a dragon. They asked me to be a dragon. "I'm not a dragon, I'm a bus driver," I said.

"Aw, be a dragon for us!"

Finally I agreed to be a dragon. I didn't let on that I had changed into a dragon. I just suddenly let out a roar that shook the bus. They screamed. Boy, how they screamed. You could hear them all over the place. It was scary. For me. It sounded like I was torturing them. "Do it again! Do it again!" they yelled. "Be a dragon again!"

So I did. I let out another roar. This time, when they screamed, teachers came running. It really did sound like something bad had happened. By the time teachers started piling in the door, the kids were laughing hysterically. I roared again. They screamed again. The teachers covered their ears and backed down the stairs. It was almost the end of the school year, and they had had enough. They didn't have to hear this. This was my doing; I could have it. The teachers left. The other kids came. We all left. I felt very good about my performance as a dragon.

When spring comes onto the valleys and hills, it is special, and when the flowers are out and the hay is growing young and green in the fields and the sky is blue above and your dog is waiting for you at the end of your driveway, and he's jumping up and down with happiness at seeing you once more, there might not be anything better in the world. All kids should have dogs waiting for them. Or cats. But cats can't, or won't, jump up and down for joy like dogs can.

June, 2009

June was amazing. Each day was rare; each day was countable; each day brought us closer to the end of the school year.

June 1st was a really hot day. I made the mistake of trying to fool with Earl. "Earl," I said, "you know, all the instruction I had, nobody ever taught me how to turn on the air conditioner."

Earl studied me for a couple of seconds, and then said, "Come on out. Let's look at your bus." We went out to where I had parked the bus outside the garage.

"Okay," said Earl, studying old Phil. "Let's see. I believe you have a Model 2550. I can tell that by the number of windows. Count 'em up. See, you have 23 windows and two top hatches. Here's what you do. Get in the bus, open all the windows and the top hatches. Got it?"

"Yeah..."

"Get behind the wheel, start 'er up, drive down to the Interstate, get on it, bring her up to 50 mph, and there you go! Model 2550. Real easy system to operate. Very few moving parts. You shouldn't have too much trouble with it."

And with that, Earl turned on his heel and went back into the garage.

On June 2nd there was a woman on the radio promoting a theory that children were too restricted in their play these days; that they should be allowed more unsupervised time to themselves. Free Range Children, she called her proposition. She stated that statistics showed that during the past thirty years, instances of predation of young children had dropped significantly, while restrictive laws had grown out of proportion to the problem. Thinking back over the past year, watching the concerned looks on parents' faces as they put their kids on the bus or met them when they came home, my thought was: tell it to the Marines. I think she missed the point. Maybe the reason for less predation was the institution of new laws? But there she was, spouting this inane theory for all the world to hear. Well, that's the Constitution for you. Let 'er rip.

June 3rd: the Mountain Gazette reported that Kevin Spacey and Scott (No Country For Old Men) Rudin would co-produce the Captain Phillips movie for Columbia.

June 4th: a teacher in Philadelphia threw a stapler at a student who was standing in the doorway of his room talking to a friend. The unruly student refused to move when instructed to do so. The teacher lost it and threw the stapler, which bounced off the wall and hit the student in the head. Blood all over. Four stitches. Things like this happen when the weight of the year is just too much to take. Some people want the school year to extend for the entire year. I say whoever proposes that should be assigned immediately as a teacher somewhere, anywhere, and let him do what teachers do during the current school year. Then he can be released from his teaching contract and allowed to conduct a press conference, so we could see if his notions had changed any. This assumes he still has the ability to put two sentences together and isn't foaming at the mouth.

June 5th: I spent an hour in the middle of the day unfastening and lifting seats, examining them for signs of gum and any structural defects. I detected a green gum aficionado in the vicinity of Seat 20. I mentioned this on the way home, to general hilarity and shouts of "He got ya, Fiona!" That was easy.

June 6th: D-Day observed.

June 8th: exam week began. This meant a shortened schedule, getting the senior high schoolers at noon, all that. It also meant that the entire district could feel everything winding down.

June 9th: Backwards Day at Underhill Central School, and it really was fun to watch as the kids got off the bus, turned around, and walked backwards down the path and into the building. Not one of them tripped on the curb, either. I don't know how that could not happen.

June 10th: I turned the bus over to the kindy-gartners and first graders on the Jericho run. They all immediately ran to the back seats and kicked out the third and fourth graders, who had to come up to the front and sit there. The little ones were ecstatic. At last! Power!

June 11th: Silly Hat Day at the elementary schools.

June 12th: I was assigned to drive Underhill Central third and fourth graders, parents, teachers, lunches, projects, and such to the Fairbanks Museum in St. Johnsbury, all the way over on the eastern side of the state. It was a long trip. Took almost two hours to get there. Before we left, Alan gave me a Mapquest route and told me to follow it. "So we'll know where you are when you break down," he said.

We left Underhill Central at 8:15 AM and headed east. A long time later we arrived at St. J. I dropped everyone at the museum, declined an invitation to accompany them, parked the bus, and gave myself my own little mini-vacation. I went to the St. J library—the Athenaeum, it's called—and toured the artwork and sculptures there. I recommend it to you if you are anywhere in the St. J vicinity. It is remarkable. It was constructed in 1871 by Horace Fairbanks, of the Fairbanks Scales Fairbanks. It is a beautiful building. It has a collection of 100 paintings, mostly originals from the Hudson Valley School, with some copies of VanDycks, Raphaels, Rembrandts, and the like thrown in for variety. It also has a collection of 40,000 volumes, which is enough to keep anyone busy for a couple of hours.

I viewed the stunning Victorian building and the extraordinary art collection, then chose a table in a cool, quiet room and made notes for this volume. I treated myself to lunch, wandered about the town, sat on a park bench and kept an eye on the bus, and at 2:30 I picked up the expedition at the museum and headed west into the sunset. We arrived back at the school at 4:30 or so. A great cheer went up when we sighted the school. One of the parents complimented me on my driving but added, "The next time we go there, we'll take a plane." Well, yes, four hours on a school bus in the middle of a hot summer day is a little bit longer than you want to be on there, even with all the windows and hatches open and the Model 2550 air conditioning system blasting away at full throttle.

June 15th: the last day of school.

June 16th: a half day, for make-up exams. There were just a few students taking make-up exams, so we were able to devote our full attention to The Cookout. As at the beginning of school, the garage was set up with tables, and Earl and Jon and Craig flipped burgers on grills set up outside. Many of the drivers contributed dishes. All the road crews from the towns we served were invited, and they came and ate hamburgers and sipped Coke with us. Then we went home.

June 17th: The Washing of the Bus. This was the final cleaning of the year, inside and out, and if you did it right, it took four or more hours to do it. I will not describe it further. Just hope you never have to do it. But, all things considered, it is a fitting ending to the school year.

Bedrock

Well, here we are at the end of the saga.

I cannot end, however, without a salute to the amazing students I drove during this most eventful year, and an equally heartfelt salute to the men and women of the Chittenden East Supervisory District Department of Transportation.

Over the year, I met extraordinary people: drivers, mechanics, cafeteria workers, custodians, road crews, firemen, police, teachers-aides—all of them the bedrock upon which this nation operates. They do their jobs quietly for the most part, out of the limelight. They do those jobs well. They rise early and make sure that everything is all set to go before the rest of the world gets out of bed. They make the day. They take pride in their work. They are seldom recognized. They are seldom paid what they are worth. Without them, society could not function.

And what can I say about the students? They were terrific, all of them. They made this a special year for me. And now they are all moving on, up a grade, out into the wider world.

...So I will sit here and watch our present-day Argonauts as they row their big yellow ship into the future. They ply their oars faster, more erratically than we would want them to. Closer to the shoals. Daring the waters. Forward to their destiny. Completing our destiny. Down to the rim of the sky. Down to the answer why. Into the clouds of infinity. There they go...

...and the bus rolls on...

Acknowledgements

I could not have completed this work without the encouragement and expert guidance of my publisher/editor from The Tamarac Press, Pat Goudey O'Brien. I have a myriad of other individuals to thank, as well. Jennifer Salmon's cover art and interior sketches are priceless. A picture is worth a thousand words, right? The legal guidance of Cindy Ellen Hill, Esq., was invaluable. So was the input of Bob Magee, Supervisor of Transportation for the Chittenden East Supervisory District, and the other drivers, mechanics, and support staff at the transportation division. Especially helpful were my trainers, Craig Moody and Alan Salter. Always there was encouragement and interest from the parents of students and from the students themselves. And underlying all the process was the constant understanding, encouragement and review of my wife, Joan Bowker, who makes the music that makes the whole thing worthwhile.

An Invitation

I would like to extend an invitation to all school bus drivers, ex-school bus drivers, parents of kids on school buses, kids on school buses, teachers and anyone else out there who has a great story, to contact me and submit that story. If we get enough of them, we (I mean you who are reading this and myself) can perhaps create a second volume of "A Year on the Bus," incorporating stories from all over the United States and beyond. Contact me at 11highmeadow@comcast.net or on www.thetamaracpress.com.

Happy and Safe Driving! I hope you enjoyed the book.

About the Author

Dan Close's background in education includes teaching in a variety of places on the globe, including Long Island, Manhattan, the Bronx, St. Croix in the U.S. Virgin Islands, at Shiprock in Navajoland, and at over 9,000 feet in altitude in the little mountain town of Bekoji, fabled home of Ethiopia's long-distance runners.

Now he resides in Underhill, Vermont, where in retirement he runs a combination one-room schoolhouse and twice-daily homeroom commonly known as a school bus. He enjoys every minute of it. Well, almost every minute. The rest of his time is taken up with tending a garden (anybody want a zucchini?), stacking wood, chopping kindling, listening to his wife play her harp, writing, traveling, and wondering what is going to happen next.

Dan can be reached at: 11highmeadow@comcast.net

Bus Documents

Daily Inspection Report

SCHOOL BUS VEHICLE PRE-TRIP INSPECTION REPORT
Mt. Mansfield Union School District

BUS #__________ ODOMETER READING____________
DATE____________ TIME__________ Location__________

Run starting time____________
Elem arrival time____________
MMU arrival time____________

INSPECT ITEMS LISTED...
...IF DEFECTIVE CIRCLE/CHECK AND DESCRIBE IN 'REMARKS'

___FLUID LEAKS UNDER BUS
___LOOSE WIRES, HOSE CONNECTIONS,
___BELTS IN ENGINE COMPARTMENT
___OIL LEVEL
___RADIATOR COOLANT LEVEL
___STEERING & BRAKE FLUIDS
___TRANSMISSION
___GUAGES & WARNING LIGHTS
___SWITCHES, PANEL AREA
___UNUSUAL ENGINE NOISE
___PARKING BRAKE-SERVICE BRAKE
___WIPERS & WASHERS & HORN
___FANS & DEFROSTERS
___STOP ARM CONTROL (WARNING)
___INSIDE/OUTSIDE MIRRORS
___BREAK PEDAL - WARNING LIGHT
___SERVICE DOOR
___EMERGENCY EQUIPMENT
___FIRST AID KIT
___CLEANLINESS OF INTERIOR

___DIRECTIONAL & PARKING LIGHTS
___HEADLIGHTS, 8-LIGHT SYS, 4-WAYS
___RT FRONT TIRE,WHEEL,SPRING,BRAKE
___FRONT OF BUS & WINDSHIELD
___LFT FRONT TIRE,WHEEL,SPRING,BRAKE
___STOP ARM, ALL CLEARANCE LIGHTS
___EXHAUST SYSTEM, TAIL PIPE
___BUS LEFT SIDE-WINDOWS & LIGHTS
___LEFT REAR TIRES & WHEELS
___REAR OF BUS-WINDOWS - LIGHTS
___BATTERY
___RIGHT REAR TIRES & WHEELS
___BUS RIGHT SIDE-WINDOWS & LIGHTS
___DRIVER'S SEAT AND BELT
___EMERGENCY EXITS & BUZZERS
___PARKING BRAKE - SERVICE BRAKE
___CLUTCH
___STEERING
___ENTRANCE STEPS
___CONDITION OF FLOOR

REMARKS____

CONDITIONS OF ABOVE VEHICLE IS: ___SATISFACTORY ___UNSATISFACTORY

DRIVER'S SIGNATURE________________________________

++

___ ABOVE DEFECTS CORRECTED

___ ABOVE DEFECTS NEED NOT BE CORRECTED FOR SAFE OPERATION OF VEHICLE

MECHANIC'S SIGNATURE____________________ DATE____________

Bus Driver ID

Inspection Procedure, page 1

PRE-TRIP INSPECTION

As you approach the bus, do visual check for any obvious defects. I.e.: vandalism, broken windows, flat tires, broken lights.

Front of bus:
Check:

Running lights at top
School bus letters
Light covers and hoods over lights
Windshield and wipers
Inspection sticker – March, August, and December
Hood
Directional lights and covers
Grill
Headlights, directionals, casings
Mirrors and support bars
Front bumper, license plate and registration sticker

Open hood:
Check:

Coolant level
Oil level
No leaks
Hoses for cracks
Serpentine belt – no more than ½ inch of play
Air filter
Fuel filter
Radiator and fan

Suspension:
Check on passenger side:

Leaf springs and U bolts – check for cracks
Front and rear spring mounts
Shocks – no leaks
Shock mounts
I – beam – from tire to tire
Tie rod end – no play
Tie rod end knuckle
King pin – whole assembly to tire
Air hose to air brakes
Air canister
Slack adjuster – 1 inch of play
Tire – no damage
Dust cover of brake
Need flashlight to look through to check brake pads

Inspection Procedure, page 2

Tire depth – 4/32 on front, no recaps
Lug nuts – secure, not loose
Hub seal – no leaks
Mud flap

Move to driver side:
Check:
Steering arm – no more than 2 inches of play
Pitman arm
Drag link – no play
Drag link knuckle
Hoses – no cracks or rips
Transmission fluid
Steering fluid
Radiator and fan from this side
Leaf springs and U bolts
Front and rear spring mounts
Shocks – no leaks
Shock mounts
I-beam – from tire to tire
Tie rod end – no play
Tie rod end knuckle
King pin – whole assembly to tire
Air hose to air brakes
Air canister
Slack adjuster – 1 inch of play
Tire
Dust cover for brake
Need flashlight to look through to check brake pads
Tire depth – 4/32 on front, no recaps
Rims & lug nuts – secure
Hub seal – no leaks
Mud flap

Driver side of bus:
Check:
Foot pegs
Mirrors – secure, not cracked
Stop sign – secure, lights not cracked or missing
Running lights
Windows – no cracks or breaks
Reflectors
Emergency exits – clearly marked, reflector tape present
No damage to exterior of bus
Battery box – door functions, battery secure, wires – no damage or cracks

Inspection Procedure, page 3

Rear duals – nothing lodged in or between, tire depth 2/32 and can run recaps
Air pressure – visual
Rims and lug nuts - secure
Hub seal – no leaks
Springs and mounts
Slack adjuster
Hoses
Fuel cage – secure, no damage
Fuel tank – secure, no damage or leaks
Fuel door – opens properly
Fuel cap - secure
Overflow hose – secure, no damage or leaks
Lights and reflectors
Exterior of bus – no damage
Windows – no damage
Doors – no damage, opens properly
Glass- no damage
Handle – works properly

Inside:
Check:

- Railing on stair – secure
- Door light – cover is not broken
- Stairway – no obstructions, in good condition
- Safety equipment –
  - First aid kit – securely mounted
  - Fire extinguisher – 5 pound, ABC, 2004, securely mounted
  - Triangles and flares
  - Extra fuses and breakers
  - Seat belt – no rips, functions properly
- Trash can – must be secured to the floor

Walk through bus:
Check:

- Seat backs and seats – secure, no rips
- Seat belts – securely installed
- Floor – no damage or debris
- Emergency exits – open properly and buzzer sounds
- Back door – opens properly and buzzer sounds
- Roof emergency exit – opens properly and buzzer sounds

Front inside:
Check:

- Driver's seat – secure to floor
- Steering wheel – no more than 2 inches of play
- Check all switches – function properly

Inspection Procedure, page 4

Underneath:
Check:

- Look for puddles under bus indicating any leaking fluids
- Oil pan
- Transmition pan
- Hoses
- Air dryer
- Exhaust and hangers – secure, no holes
- Drive shaft and hangers
- Frame – no cracks or damage
- Floor supports – no cracks or damage
- Air tank
- Slack adjusters on rear next to air canister
- Hoses in rear end
- Rear spring mounts
- U bolts
- Inside dual – nothing lodged in or between
- Rear tire depth – 2/32, can use recaps, no cracks or damage
- Air pressure - visual
- Rims &lug nuts – secure
- Hub seal – no leaks
- Rear shock
- Mud flap
- Rear end
- Frame
- Floor supports

Back of bus:
Check:

- Look for signs of damage – i.e.: broken windows or lights, dents, vandalism
- Running lights
- Black lettering
- Lights, covers and reflectors
- Emergency exit – door functions well
- Door seal around inside of door
- License and registration sticker
- Bumper
- Exhaust – secure and round, extends 1 inch beyond bumper

Passenger side of bus:
Check:

- Frame and floor supports
- Exhaust
- Springs and mounts
- Shocks and mounts
- Mud flap

Inspection Procedure, page 5

Horn
Seat belt
Lights – high beam and low beams – be sure high beam indicator works
Directionals
4 way hazard lights
8 ways and stop sign
Brake lights
Parking lights
Reverse lights and warning signal

Air Brake Test:

Bus is not running but key is ON! Parking brake needs to be off, wheels need to be chocked. Hold foot on brake for one minute to show that the bus will not lose more than 3 psi in 1 minute.
After 1 minute, pump brake to release air until gauge reaches 60 psi – warning light should come on.
Then pump brake until pressure reaches 20 psi – parking brake should come on.
Start bus – check gauges while air pressure goes back up. You can depress the accelerator slightly to increase the air pressure. Wait until air pressure goes back up and then blows off.

Check emergency brake:

Be sure emergency brake is still on from air brake test. Remove chocks from tires, put bus in gear and step on gas – bus should not move!

Bus Idling Law

NO. 48. AN ACT RELATING TO THE IDLING OF MOTOR VEHICLE ENGINES ON SCHOOL PROPERTY

(S. 13)

It is hereby enacted by the General Assembly of the State of Vermont:

Sec. 1. 23 V.S.A. § 1282(f/ is added to read:

(f) Subject to state board of education rules, which may provide for limited idling, the operator of a school bus shall not idle the engine while waiting for children to board or to exit the vehicle at a school and shall not start the engine until ready to leave the school premises. The board, in consultation with the agency of natural resources, the department of health, and the department of motor vehicles, shall adopt rules to implement this subsection. The rules shall set forth periods or circumstances that reasonably require the idling of the engine, including periods when it is necessary to operate defrosting, heating, or cooling equipment to ensure the health or safety of the driver or passengers or to operate auxiliary equipment; and periods when the engine is undergoing maintenance or inspection.

Sec. 2. SCHOOL BOARDS AND VEHICULAR IDLING:

Nothing in this act or in department of education rules shall prevent a school board from adopting idling policies for motor vehicles other than school buses when present on school premises. by January 1, 2008, the department of education shall develop a model policy relating to idling of vehicles other than school buses to be distributed to schools for their use.

Sec. 3. EFFECTIVE DATE:

This act shall take effect on paasage. The rules required by this act shall take effect during the 2007-2008 academic year.

Approved: May 25, 2007

www.ingramcontent.com/pod-product-compliance
Lightning Source LLC
Chambersburg PA
CBHW072146130726
47909CB00004BB/1244

9780970662026